1

THE TERRIBLE LOYALTY

A quest inspired by Robin Lee Graham's 'Dove'

Honorable Mention awards:
Eric Hoffer Independent Book Award 2014
Paris Book Festival 2013
New York Book Festival 2013
Hollywood Book Festival 2013
San Francisco Book Festival 2013
The Beach Book Festival 2013

Printing: May 2014

ISBN 978-1477651551

THE TERRIBLE LOYALTY

A quest inspired by Robin Lee Graham's 'Dove'

Sandy Moss

www.mossycovepublications.com

TABLE OF CONTENTS:

To the brave men and women through the ages who have taken on the sea as friend and adversary, including these two.

1
Genesis of the Journey

The raging sea pounded the sides of the small boat with a vengeance that threatened to tear it apart. Shep ducked a cold torrent of ocean water that tore across the starboard deck to disappear in the churning water on the other side. His stomach heaved as erratically as the twenty-foot sailboat that tossed beneath him. But it wasn't the storm that scared him. It was what it would mean if he didn't make it through. All the things back home he hadn't finished. All the love he'd left undone.

It was his idea as much as Dave's to take this trip across the Pacific Ocean from the verdant southern end of California to the even-greener mountains of Hilo, Hawaii. It was a testing of manhood, perhaps, but of life really. So, if it didn't turn out well, he had only himself to blame, not the man struggling with a drag chute on the other end of the boat. In Shep's mind, no matter the cost, this was the choice he'd wanted.

Dave was the sailor, Shep the land crab. As a youngster, Dave had sensed the ebb and flow of the sea in his veins. Before he found an ocean upon which to sail, he'd spent his winters trudging to the top of the local neighborhood hill with his blue Radio Flyer wagon bumping behind. At the highest point, right there in front of old Mrs. Peterson's faded yellow clapboard house with the peeling paint and the now-brown wisteria, he'd turn the small wagon backwards so its metal tongue served as a rudder of sorts, then crawl aboard and with skinny legs hanging over each side, begin his flying descent. Past all the houses of his friends safe inside watching black-and-white reruns of The Lone Ranger, he'd sail that shiny cart like the sailboat he wished it was, down, down, down, till he ran out of hill and the magnificent sailing vessel became once again just a little blue wagon rolling soundlessly into his own driveway.

It wouldn't be until years later that Dave would see the full portent of his wagon-sailing adventures and realize the depth of commitment he had to being on the sea, "come hell or high water," as his long-dead grandmother used to say.

Shep's commitment to crossing the ocean was not because he loved the sea. He didn't. Anything that made him feel over his head or out of control was almost unbearably uncomfortable. He wanted to travel the vastness of the Pacific Ocean at its loneliest point because it was The Great Adventure. It was something few men did in a lifetime, something that would test a man's mettle against a vastness that seemed empty, but indeed was full of life and promise. Perhaps like the universe itself.

Shep had sailed before on the ocean. At university in California, he'd even owned a sailboat, though he knew in his heart of hearts he'd never really be a sailor. Not like Dave, and not like one of his heroes, Captain Ahab of Moby Dick, both men of strength and unfailing determination. No, Shep was a sailor of kites, not ships.

As a boy, while Dave was sailing his Radio Flyer down a long Spokane hill, Shep was making kites from newspaper and leftover string: Kites the size of a postage stamp or kites the size of a small billboard that would sail at the end of his fingertips up, up, and farther up, until even the largest looked like an insect against the blue Arizona sky. A string, a wind, and something flat were the only things he truly knew of sailing. Never in Shep's wildest imagination, and he certainly had one of those, did he think that someday he'd find himself on a twenty-foot fiberglass sailboat with a dove and a cross stamped high on its white sail, setting off for a far-away island across thousands of miles of austere sea. Nor did Dave, for that matter, but he felt it was God's challenge to him to cross the sea. He felt so strongly that it was his destiny that even if he died it would be okay.

Neither Shep nor Dave could know what this voyage would mean to them, how it would change who they were and what they dreamed.

2
Plans for the Crossing

David Chamberlain and Michael "Shep" Shepard had been friends for a very long time. Not just friends, but brothers...brothers of a larger bond than blood: brothers of devotion and of the cloth. This trip was their Radical Sabbatical, their retreat from the world for a testing of faith and friendship. They'd taken to calling it, "The Terrible Loyalty," after a quote by Catholic convert and English theologian, G. K. Chesterton, which had hung on a foyer wall in the small church where Shep had his first pastoral flock.

We are all in the same boat on a stormy sea, and we owe each other a terrible loyalty.

The two men could have no idea then how accurate that quote would come to be.

This ocean voyage was also a 40th birthday gift for both of them, each two score years and hoping for more. The vision of the 2,500-mile sailing trip was born in a moment before they saw those four decades stacking up before them.

A little more than a year before, while Dave was attending a pastor's enclave in the San Francisco area, up from his home in Chula Vista, he'd dropped over to spend the evening with Shep. For all their attachment and friendship, the two men hadn't seen each other for several years. After a long day of meetings and work the two were finally comfortably ensconced on the front porch of Shep's Redwood City home. With ice melting and snapping in their iced tea the two talked and laughed, catching up season by season on each other's lives. Before long, the conversation swung around to how fast the years were passing.

"We'll be 40 next year!" Dave said, giving his tea a swirl.

"We ought to do something great -- something special," Shep said, never content to have life passing him by with no great defining moments. "As a matter of fact, maybe it's time to cross the Pacific Ocean."

For years, the two had talked of making an ocean sojourn together, but as daydreams go, so far nothing had come of it.

"You know, Dave, we can dream of The Great Adventure until we're 90, but all the talk is worthless unless we actually do it," Shep continued, as their rockers gently squeaked back and forth, rivaling the crickets' songs in the bushes.

"Yes," Dave agreed, gazing unseeing into the dark beyond the porch. "Better to do it than to be old and gray and sitting in our easy chairs telling our grandchildren we once *thought* of doing a brave and solitary thing."

Laughing, he added, "It'll be the perfect mid-life crisis."

And so it was that warm night in May, 1991, with a firmament of stars riding above the porch roof as far as the eye could see, the two old friends committed themselves to crossing the mighty ocean together exactly

one year from that date, neither fathoming what a turn
their fates could take.

3
Two Very Different Boys

During his childhood, Shep had not traveled more than a hundred miles from his small hometown of Prescott, Arizona. He'd spent his days with neighborhood friends building forts, manning wrecked automobile hoods down the backsides of creeks, or rescuing swallows fallen from their nest.

He didn't see the ocean until he was nine. He knew it existed, of course, from photos and stories his Navy veteran father had told him. Then, that summer of '62, he took a trip to San Francisco with an older couple, Horace and Bobbie Mitchell, who "fostered" him at their farm in Chino Valley during those three months without school. When Shep saw that vast expanse of surging blue-green water, he was awestruck by its sheer size, its crashing waves and the pungent smell of its salty sea life.

But while fascinated with the ocean, Shep would do no more than dab his bare toes in the creeping foam as the water sought the shore. Afraid to embrace the endlessness of the ocean so far from his native environment, he felt more than a slight discomfort at the beach and had no yearning to venture beyond the shoreline.

"Go ahead, Shep. Get in that salty water!" Bobbie encouraged. "It's fun!"

Shep turned to her as she spoke, then looked back toward the thrash of the waves on the sand and shook his head resolutely, "no."

Even on sweltering days with his pals in Prescott, Shep would very rarely venture into a pond or pool. He hung back, watching the other boys splashing with abandon, not jealous, but hesitant, unsure of the safety of such an ephemeral thing as water. He would not know until years later that his penultimate best friend loved water in every form. Dave was always the first one in, diving, jumping, flipping into the cool liquid with alacrity. A true Aquarian, though born a Libra, an air sign, he was not only a man of the land, but inherently at home on the sea.

While young Shep was planting sunflower seeds and watching with scarce-contained enthusiasm for them to sprout tender leaves, Dave was venturing onto lakes with a homemade skiff. As Shep was taking his care-grown flowers to the county fair, or raising chickens for a Boy Scout project, Dave was mastering the art of sailing, launching model rockets, or memorizing constellations.

But when the boy born to sail and the Arizona mountain boy met, there was an inexplicable magic of friendship between them from the first hello.

4

Shep in San Francisco

Some young men might have been nervous on this, their first day of a new life, the beginning, in fact, of the most important part of the rest of their life, but not so with Shep. He was gregarious, enthusiastic, more comfortable with people than without them. So the dozens of boys crammed together in the big San Francisco Salvation Army Officer's Training gym, that smelled of sweaty socks and even sweatier bodies, was just his cup of tea.

Shep was 18. His thick black hair was touched with a hint of curl, his dusky skin spoke of a Mexican mother and Scottish father. Dark eyes set in a handsome face missed nothing. He saw the long tables manned by teachers and loaded with stacks of books. Books whose lofty contents he would, no doubt, be required to read and eventually recite on test after test.

He saw the San Francisco sun slanting in bright lines from the grids of tall windows, falling softly on the gleaming gym floor and thought of home and the quality of light in the town he'd left behind, its muted colors of gold and bronze warming the historic houses and quaint downtown shops.

Shep also remembered his reasons for being here: To become a spokesman for God. To learn the interpretations of scriptures from the great minds of the world so he could shepherd the lambs to the fold, as his Scottish surname implied.

Since a babe in arms, being a minister is what Shep had been destined to do. His wizened and devout Catholic grandmother had touched his dark curls on the day he was born and pronounced that, "This child is to be the holy man of the family." Shep had never questioned that calling, nor had his family. After all, hadn't he always been the one who was the entertainer, ever the performer? As a small boy, Shep had sought the spotlight of attention from friends, family and acquaintances. When his parents would go visiting, Shep would inevitably be lifted to a dining table or couch where he would soft shoe his way into the hearts of anyone watching, strumming an air guitar and singing Elvis Presley's, "Let Me Be Your Teddy Bear," or other such adult song better suited for children.

Shep also thought of a different light, the rainbow light thrown from the rows of tall, stained glass windows at the ancient Sacred Heart Church on Marina Street in Prescott where he had been an altar boy for all the years of his youth. That light had filtered down upon his white robe as he had lit the candles and carried the host every Sunday. It was that light that had brought him here. As a grown man now, he was willing and ready to take the next step toward his calling. No longer a Catholic, the Salvation Army Officers' Training School was Shep's touchstone, the place he was meant to be.

A tall and charismatic young man, J.R. Rocheleau, had acquainted him with the Salvation Army when he came to Prescott High School during Shep's junior year, after moving from Clovis, New Mexico. The boys' passion for Volkswagen Beetles and girls had forged a tight bond between them.

J.R.'s parents, former Canadians John and Mary, had discovered the Army in their native land then came to the U.S. to pursue their mission. When Shep began attending the Salvation Army's Sunday services with J.R., he decided he rather liked its point of view, not to mention admiring its long ago founder, William Booth from 1860's England. Booth was a fearless man of God who'd ministered to the poor and hungry at a time when the industrial revolution had dehumanized the masses.

While women weep as they do now, I'll fight; while little children go hungry as they do now, I'll fight; while there yet remains one dark soul without the light of God, I'll fight. I'll fight to the very end, Booth had said.

Those powerful and compassionate words spoke to Shep's soul. He abandoned the church of his fathers and became a Protestant, though forever remaining a proud ethnic Catholic in his heart.

5

Beginning of a Friendship

Registration completed, Shep wandered into the seminary lobby, picked his room assignment card from the alphabetized list and consulted a wall map. Room 26c in the men's dorm wing would be his home-away-from-home for the next two years. Slinging his bulky clothing bag over his shoulder and muscling his worn suitcase from its resting place on the floor near the door, Shep headed down the hallway.

"Hey, buddy," someone called out from behind him. "You have room 26?"

Hailing him was a plumpish young man with auburn hair and a cherubic face that belied a rough childhood in the Bronx.

"I'm George. George Simmons. I think I'm your roommate."

Shep smiled. Great. At least his roomy wasn't shy.

The two walked side-by-side, bags and shoulders bouncing off each other as they negotiated a hallway built more comfortably for only one pack animal.

Rooms passed, every one a carbon copy of the other on this first day before posters and bulletin boards covered the walls, or plaid or colored spreads decked the narrow twin beds clinging to opposite walls.

Shep noticed one boy in particular already settled in a room. The boy was a standout because he, like Shep, had hair visibly longer than acceptable regulation. As its name implied, The Salvation Army could indeed be a bit like the military, complete with uniforms, hair cropped to 1960's respectable length and reveille at 6 a.m. sharp each and every morning.

Making a note to look that kid up later, Shep and Georgie Porgie, (already nicknamed by Shep), struggled on to their room down the hall. Shep dumped his belongings on the left bed, which designated the right-hand bed for George. Shep could see that the small closet near the foot of his bed would be plenty big for his two suit coats, the selection of starched, collared shirts his mother had packed, and the few dress slacks he'd bought at J.C. Penney's before leaving town.

Worn brown dressers flanked the closets and would suffice for the Army's regulation white T-shirts and a jumble of socks and shorts. Quickly emptying his suitcase and stowing it beneath the iron bed frame, Shep scoped out the view from the second-story room. There, spread below like E.M. Forster's, "Room with a View," was a 180-degree panorama of "The City," San Francisco in the flesh, where he'd spend the next twenty-four months learning his life's profession. Full of restless energy, Shep headed out to explore the rest of the dorm.

"Hi, I'm Michael Shepard," he greeted the longhaired kid in Room 36. "You can call me Shep."

"I'm David Chamberlain," replied the tall, thin boy with the sandy-colored hair and emerald eyes.

The two boys were reverse images of the other, the light-haired one and the dark one, but an instant magnetism sprung up between them, not just because of their equally long tresses, but because of something more, some indescribable inner thing that can define friendship, or love, or life-long companions. The two had found a small, but identifiable refuge in the midst of a sea of strangers, something to grasp onto, if ever so slightly.

"I think we have a mutual problem here," Dave said, taking the words out of the air between them.

"Our hair's too long," they laughed in unison.

"You have scissors?" Shep asked.

Male adolescents of nineteen are generally not prone to trust anyone to cut their hair, least of all a stranger, hair being a most well-guarded commodity in the regular world of girls, cars, and dating, a thing that defines the cool guys from the not-so-savvy ones. But this was their brave new world, somewhere different from any place they'd been before. The newness compelled them to a fast assessment and an instant trust of each other.

Dave produced a semi-dull pair of scissors from his recently arranged desk drawer, a comb from the small cubby of a bathroom, then sat on a worn wooden chair with knees tight together awaiting his fate. Brave beyond his experience, Shep gingerly lifted a lock of hair the color of sunburned mangoes from the top of Dave's head and snipped it off…then another, and another. An hour later, looking like sheep having suffered a frightening shearing, the boys emerged from the room to congregate with several hundred of their new comrades in the dining hall for their first dinner of many together.

Dave Chamberlain and Mike "Shep" Shepard

Shep and Dave were friends now. Oddly enough, they even wore the same size clothes and shoes. Many were the times when Dave would look up from his books, only to see Shep entering class wearing one of Dave's favorite shirts or jackets.

"Dang it, Shep," he'd say, "you could at least ask!"

It irked him, though he knew it shouldn't. Shep was like an Indian. He had no boundaries. What was his was yours and he just assumed it was the other way around, too. Reigning in his natural possessiveness, Dave knew it was really more important what the two had in common. It just seemed like he and Shep could talk for hours on end on a thousand subjects. They'd zoom to the past, speed to the present, or project light years ahead into the future to their gray-haired days and still understand each other. Their thoughts seemed transparent to each other. Neither boy had ever had a friend quite like the other. Most significantly of all, they could endure magnificent mutual silences, the true test of friendship. They were also young men with the same mission for their lives -- to serve God. Each understood that great commission and had now found someone who understood it with the same crystal clarity.

Two years later, after having seldom been apart, the two young men would be even closer friends and would remain so far beyond the day they would march solemnly down the graduation aisle toward a very different life.

6

The Yoyo Incident

A s the golden leaves fluttered from fall trees, Dave and Shep polished the gold of their new friendship. Both unique, of commanding presence, fun-loving and competitive, the two seemed almost to have a single identity with staff and fellow cadets to such a degree that years later, when the magic would on occasion go stale at the seminary, one of the staff members could be heard to remark, "What the officers training school needs is another Dave and Shep around. They always made sure everyone was having a good time."

The two were sanguine personality types, and rather like otters, loved to entertain and be entertained. If nothing is happening, a sanguine will make sure it changes. So it was on one crisp autumn day, Dave came across a giant yoyo in some novelty shop in the back haunts of San Francisco. The size of a 45rpm record, it was made of heavy varnished maple. Looming big on its face was a pasted-on logo, now worn illegible. Other than its size, the yoyo was nothing unusual. It was most likely some type of rejected souvenir from a Sausalito toy store, surely more what a circus clown would use than a person practicing the fine art of "yo'ing."

"Hey, Shep, look what I found," Dave chortled, on his return to the dorm.

"Dang, that is the biggest yo I have ever seen," Shep said, sufficiently awed.

Holding it up to the light, Shep noted with disappointment that it had only a minimal amount of string tethered to its central axle.

"You know, Dave, I think a yoyo of this size could easily accommodate 10- or 15-feet of string," Shep said.

If only one were tall enough to operate it, he mused.

"Yeah, probably," Dave replied, losing interest for the moment and taking off to check on some test results.

Shep quickly re-rigged the yoyo with a much longer piece of braided nylon string. Hurrying to the fire exit door down the hall from his room, Shep stepped briskly onto the second-story escape platform. With a flick of his wrist he let the yoyo fly.

The mega-sized yoyo zoomed down with all the force of earth's gravity below it. Quickly reaching its outer limit, the yoyo cairned noiselessly back to Shep's waiting hand. With another crisp snap, Shep sent the giant gyroscopic orb sailing back down again. After a couple of runs, he tired of the new reach and took the yoyo back to his room to examine it once more.

No matter how far it goes down, Shep theorized, it would gain enough momentum to reverse itself completely back into the thrower's hand.

That decided, Shep figured this yoyo could still accommodate more string…probably 25- to 30-feet. With more care this time, he re-rigged the yoyo with his very best Boy Scout tying techniques, making sure it had just the right amount of loop at the end so it could "sleep" before his finger signaled it back to the top.

The only down side of the operation, he thought briefly, was that catching the yoyo on the way back up could possibly be an effort requiring Catfish Hunter and his thick catcher's mitt. But undaunted, Shep tightened up the string then went in search of witnesses, who turned out to be a number of fellow cadets from rooms 14, 16, and 27, and Dave, of course, who had returned from his errand. The half-dozen curious boys joined Shep on the landing for this historic moment.

As it happened, the fire escape landing was directly above a sloping driveway which, San Francisco style, descended steeply to the street, making certain parts of the driveway much deeper than others in relation to the platform where the eager boys stood. Nearby, but not directly beneath them, was one of the school's transport vans complete with red Salvation Army logos on doors and back panels.

Shep poised himself like some high roller in Las Vegas, legs apart, hands balled as if preparing to roll against the house for a million dollars. Waiting for the precise theatrical moment when the audience could stand it no longer, with a sudden upward motion, heaving his shoulders high about his neck and springing up like a tennis pro serving, Shep swung his arm down and released the yoyo like a cannonball. Down, down, down, it went in a splendid arc. Wide-eyed, the boys watched the spinning orb begin its journey. It whined down at the speed of light, then, just as the magnificent yoyo reached its conclusion at the end of the string, it veered in slightly toward the building and, in the blink of an eye, soundly struck the roof of the shiny personnel van. A collective gasp escaped from the boys watching above. Heedless of its error, the yoyo bounced immediately up, caught its own slack on the string and reeled towards the second-floor landing. Slowing, its energy spent, the yoyo barely reached Shep's waiting hand. He turned to his audience, the oversized toy tenderly cradled in his hands. The boys gathered around ogling it as if it were a golden egg.

"Wow! Did you see that?!" one awestruck cadet whispered.

Pale with shock, Dave glared over their heads at Shep with a, *Have you lost your mind?!* look.

"See what? I didn't see anything," he said curtly, turning on his heel and feigning a nonchalant saunter into the building.

The boys' lips were sealed. The yoyo and van incident was never mentioned aloud and the fist-sized dent in the top of the white school van seemed never to have been discovered.

7

Sailing on Lake Sloan

Rigorous studies and extracurricular activities took the boys away from school on frequent assignments, but they found time to pursue other hobbies and interests as well. One eventually led them to the biggest adventure of their lives: sailing the broad band of the Pacific Ocean. It started innocently enough when Dave and Shep began building small-scale wooden ships. They scavenged wood scraps from the maintenance shop and assembled them meticulously from scratch without kits. The two had special permission from the janitor, Mr. Johnson, to use the shop after hours when the tools and workbenches sat idle. For hours on end, the young men would sit carving spars and ribs from spruce and yellow pine pieces. Salvaging buttonhole thread from private sewing kits and cotton cloth from worn-out white shirts they made rigging and sails for their miniature vessels.

Maybe he just had ships on his mind, but Dave began talking about sailing at odd moments during the day.

"Hey, we should go out on the lake together, my dry dock friend," he'd tease, shooting a basketball above Shep's head for another point.

"Oh, sure," Shep replied. "I can't even play basketball and now you want to torture me with sailing *and* being near the water!"

It did seem the two had done about everything else together -- built instruments and played music, flown kites, studied, and performed chapel services as a duo, so why not sail? Sailing was at the very heart of who Dave was, and if his best friend didn't know that part of him it would be a mighty gap.

So one sunny spring day they packed a few essentials and hopped a Muni bus. It rumbled swiftly past the business section of San Francisco then past the suburbs, but the route ended at the very edge of the city with some distance to go to Sloan Lake.

"Stick your fat thumb out there, Sheppers," Dave instructed. "We need another ride to get to the lake."

"You've got better legs than I do, sailor, why don't *you* entice the ride?" Shep bantered.

Ultimately, a guy driving an ancient Cadillac convertible and sporting sunglasses and a shirt open to his waist skidded to the roadside and beckoned them in.

"See, I told you those legs would stop a ride!" Shep laughed, as they ran to catch up to the car.

"He looks like some kind of Hunter S. Thompson clone," Dave whispered.

Once at Sloan Lake, they rented a 12-foot Oday sailboat for a whopping $4 each -- money they'd skimmed from their skimpy student budgets.

It was a perfect, windy, sailing day.

"Okay, here's how it goes," Dave instructed. "You're the slave and I'm the skipper. There's not much to figure out."

He continued briefing Shep on some minimal

sailing skills, such as how to put up the mainsail and operate the tiller.

"Heave to, buddy," he called to Shep, and boarded the boat.

"Untie us from the cleats, then jump in," he ordered good-naturedly.

The boat wobbled a bit from side to side as Shep hefted himself aboard and staggered unsteadily to his seat in the front of the cockpit. Dave manned the helm.

Once underway, the spray blew up from the skimming boat dousing Shep's face. When he looked back, his friend was sporting a big grin as the boat tacked smoothly back and forth, back and forth in the wind.

Haltingly, Shep loosened the ropes when instructed, then tightened them up, trimmed the mainsails and slid the nylon cords through the jam cleats, locking them into position.

"Ready about," Dave yelled Shep's way, telling him to echo back, "ready," so he'd know Shep had heard the command.

"Helms alee," he'd shout, whereupon Shep would quickly put his head down almost to his knees as the boom swung over, missing his head by inches on each pass, before thudding dully as the ropes went taut against the boom sheets. The boat would begin to heel in the opposite direction as it felt the wind, cutting a rugged path through the choppy water.

"This may just beat a Disneyland ride," Shep hollered to Dave, cupping his hands around his mouth and shouting back against the brisk breeze.

Echoing commands back to the skipper, Shep watched the water boiling happily around them. It was obvious to him that Dave was ever so proud to share this with him.

Dave was a sailor of experience, though much of what he knew was simply instinct and love of this sport. He'd let the boat heel completely over on its side, feeling a rush of adrenalin watching the wind flow like syrup off the sails before bringing it back upright.

That little trick scared the heck out of Shep, desert rat that he was, but it was exhilarating, too, he had to admit, a big smile lighting his tawny face.

About forty minutes into the allotted hour, a red flag appeared on a small tower by the lake's rental office.

"Oh, snakes," Dave hollered above the wind's noise to Shep.

"What's wrong?" Shep shouted back.

"Red flag conditions...that means there's too much wind," Dave called. "The Harbor Master is telling us to head back to the dock."

Disappointed, the boys tacked the small boat and headed in.

By the time they reached dock, they had been sailing fifty-nine minutes, but more than sailing had been accomplished. When Dave's hand first touched the helm that warm spring day and the boat began to move in the silky blue water, it was as if the inevitability of the transpacific crossing was written into the two young men's destiny, all the while seeming as if two college boys were just out having a day of sun and sailing.

After their experience on Lake Sloan, sailing became a new topic thrown into their box of mutual interests. They endlessly discussed different kinds of boats, equipment, and the art of sailing. One of Dave's favorite books, Robin Lee Graham's, "Dove," the story of one young boy's famous sail around the world in

1965, became Shep's favorite as well.

When Dave first gave him the book, Shep read it night after night after his studies were finished, sometimes by flashlight if it got too late and it was "lights out" time. In his busy imagination, Shep became utterly fascinated with the idea of someone taking a small boat across the entire Pacific.

So inspired were they both by sixteen-year-old Graham's brave world-sailing journey that they unconsciously put him in the category with all the martyrs and apostles of the early church that they'd learned to esteem in their studies. On that lofty foundation, they decided that they, too, would make that trip -- not around the world, that was simply too much. Instead, their dream would be more modest: only 2,500 miles in thirty days, emulating the first leg of Graham's voyage -- the sail from California to Hawaii.

Dave and Shep often talked about Graham's boat and memorized its type, class, and qualification. They even knew the modifications he'd done to prepare his boat to cross the Pacific Ocean.

Years later, when the two made that crossing themselves, they would do many of the same type of modifications to their boat. Thus rigged, their small craft that was designed to go out only two or three miles into the bay and return would be capable of crossing an endless and formidable ocean.

Without them realizing it, their grand quest had begun on their trip to Lake Sloan, born from the first sailing trip Dave and Shep ever took together and the first sailing Shep had ever done.

8

The Adventure Begins

So it was that years later, on that warm third day of May, 1992, Shep and Dave began, "The Great Adventure."

It seemed everyone the two men loved had come to see them off on their ocean crossing. Shep's entire family had gathered from across the country. His two sisters were tearful; his brother solemn; his small Mexican mother in a daze; his wife, Debby, conspicuous by her absence; and his father -- his tall, gentle father -- came because he not-so-secretly believed he'd never see his youngest son again.

The night before, the last one ashore, this small group strolled Revolution Boulevard across the border in Tijuana, Mexico. Arm-in-arm they looked in shop windows, smelled the dusty tang of the street, avoided the hawking by insistent night vendors, and peered as they passed into the open doorways of loud nightclubs where exotic molasses-skinned females danced.

The four siblings would unlock their arms and change positions like a flock of geese exchanging leaders, as they worked their way up and down the streets looking for just the right place to eat. It turned out to be

Miguel's -- Mexico's version of Golden Corral -- a family restaurant offering simple meals like the kind one puts together in one's own kitchen with cheeses, meats, spices and garnishes, making it more communal somehow.

This is much more like breaking bread than a formal dinner, Shep thought happily to himself.

Shep's father seemed even quieter than his usual laconic self that night, knowing his particular reason for being there was perhaps deeper than the rest. His apprehension about this trip seemed to belie his Depression Era survivalist mentality.

Why would anyone take this journey with the possible risks that come with it if they didn't have to, he asked himself...if it weren't a matter of life and death?

John Jacob keenly felt his own personal potential for loss in this voyage -- his beloved son -- but he couldn't deny a man's hunger for the untried. His mind wandered unbidden back all those years ago to when he had been a far younger man and he, too, yearned for adventure.

The only son of a stern Scottish-Germanic couple, at eighteen, John Jacob Shepard had untwined his two sisters' arms from his neck and jovially hopped aboard a westbound train for uncharted territory, not as a passenger, but as a stowaway. Forty years later, he still hadn't forgotten those nights in front of a boiling pot of hobo stew alongside the tracks, the colorful characters he'd met, the danger always on the edge of his mind and the feeling of the unknown always in his pocket.

Though he couldn't help but think his second son was a damned fool for embarking on this voyage, yet John remembered, too, how his heart would lurch with the train's effort to pull its heavy metal wheels from a standstill to begin its journey. As the iron horse clacked and rattled, he would think how truly lucky was this vagabond life of his. Perhaps, he thought, it was in some part his wild stories of adventure and restlessness that had given Shep this yearning to see the far side of the horizon. And because John Jacob understood Shep's wild thirst for what lay beyond the visible, he would let him go. But like his parents before him, John would also pray that Shep would come back.

"More bread, Dad?"

The question pulled John back from his past and he gazed around this foreign table at his ruddy-colored family.

Who would have guessed that this Michigan-born boy would've fallen in love with a Mexican maiden when he stopped at a small diner in southern California one early morning in the spring of 1944 for a cup of steaming coffee? There she was standing at the counter. The most beautiful woman he could ever remember seeing -- small, dark, with round sparkling eyes and rich, walnut-colored hair to her shoulders. Her name was Josie.

Unfortunately, Josie was engaged to a burly salesman of tobacco products who didn't look kindly on another man talking to his soon-to-be-bride, so John couldn't even ask her out.

Then one balmy Wednesday morning when John stopped in for coffee as usual, Josie wasn't there. Her friend Sue, who also waitressed there, said Josie had broken off her engagement, quit her job, and gone back to her home in Prescott, Arizona. Now, John Shepard may have been a quiet man, but he was not without a stubborn German streak and he simply would not let

Josie Moreno step out of his life. Within a few weeks, he had followed her to the small mountain town, knocked on the unfamiliar door and when Josie answered, insisted that she marry him, which amazingly she did with more surprise than protest.

John and Josie had been married for more than four decades now and their four children, John Lawrence, Shep, Sharon, and Deb, were all gathered at this Mexican table to see his second son off on the voyage of a lifetime.

The talk and laughter waned as they emptied their plates.

"Well, we better be heading back," Shep said.

They hailed a late-night taxi from the curb and rode crowded two-deep back to the parking area at the border.

Once settled in the comfortable motel bed, Shep couldn't sleep, though he knew his opportunity was short. Instead, he lay still as a church mouse waiting for the sun to rise, absorbed in thoughts of what lay ahead for him and anxious as a starving man for a long-promised meal.

He thought of Debby and of the children. He pictured his wife of almost seventeen years tucking ten-year-old Mandy into bed, and reading a bedtime story to little John, now eight. Surely they would have said prayers for his safety tonight.

They were never far from his mind. The very first entry in the leather-bound journal Shep would write upon his voyage, its rough red-brown front stamped with a hand-drawn fouled anchor and the word, "Pilgrimage," would read:

To John, Mandy and Debby: My heart is heavy as I set sail and watch the land melt away. I'm fearful above all of the possibility that through events yet to come, I may have seen you for the last time. It is not the width of the sea, or the depth of the ocean that scares me now. It's not the wind in a stir, or rolling waves, but a separation from you that causes me to quake inside. My most fervent prayer from here to Hilo will be, "God, let me see them again and hold them close. Till then, pray us home. Your father and husband.

Dave on the other hand, spent his last few hours ashore alone -- not with his wife and two young sons, but in his Chula Vista backyard climbing around on the journey's small sailboat. With a bare light bulb strung on a long extension cord, he checked and rechecked hatch seals and took a last look at the vessel that would take him and his best friend on a long, unforgettable sprint across the Pacific Ocean. Christened Mini, an obvious comparison to her size, Dave sensed as much as knew that the boat was seaworthy. She would be equal to the task.

9

Nice Day for a Sail

Morning came soon enough, a bright, humid May Day dawn where too many birds seemed to fill the branches of the date palms and too strident a breeze swept in from the sea. Mini perched at the edge of the ocean still latched to her sturdy trailer, but overhanging the lapping water of the bay as if anxiously awaiting her journey.

A crowd had gathered at the J-Street dock in Chula Vista. Not just family and loved ones wishing the sailors a fair sea, but the curious and the incredulous, too.

"You're doing what? You're crossing 2,500 miles of open sea in that tiny boat?" some said, shaking their heads and wondering, like the men's families, if the two could possibly survive the rigors of the mighty ocean in such a small vessel, no matter that Dave touted Mini as being, "downright roomy."

But no matter their reason for being there, each onlooker was taken with the venture, somehow as proud of the adventurers as if they were making the trip themselves.

A local newspaper had publicized the journey and local sailors came to see them off, too, fascinated by two intrepid men's determination to sail a 20-foot dinghy from the coast of California to the shores of the far-away Hawaii.

"We want to shake your hands," they said, sunburned faces tilted to the morning sun. "We wouldn't do it. We wouldn't make that trip in that boat, but we wanted to meet the men who would."

Most of the sailors had sailed hundreds of miles up the coast, but never due west. Nonetheless, they offered to tune the rigging and wrap the turnbuckles for blue-water cruising. For Shep and Dave, the well-wishes of these true sailors was even more buoying than those from the ones they held dear. It was to them the two voyagers left the work of rigging while they attended a church service with their families, much like the sailors in Moby Dick before their fateful trip.

The sailors did their job well, polishing and rubbing Mini to a fine shine as if she were a professional boxer about to bow into the ring. Not unlike trainers, they taped her jagged protrusions like the binding on a boxer's hands to see her through the bout she was to begin.

With the sun rising higher in the mild sky, at last Shep and Dave stood in Mini's cockpit surveying the crowd.

"What does this remind you of, Dave?" Shep turned aside to whisper to Dave.

At Dave's puzzled expression, he continued, "How about the Wizard of Oz getting ready to launch his magnificent balloon toward Kansas with the Munchkins dancing around and hanging on his every word?"

"Right," Dave laughed back. "Just don't let 'em see behind the curtain!"

Everything the men said was funny, eliciting

nervous titters from the crowd. The people huddled close around the boat and leaned toward them expectantly, listening intently, feeling the gravity of the occasion. But only the two men on the sailboat truly felt keen apprehension, but again, as the Wizard on the other side of curtain, they instead acted calm and all knowing. In truth, each was stunned by how fast this day had arrived and the reality of the size of the undertaking under their feet. Though they'd carefully calculated the chronology of the trip, even now they had no real sense of the actual expanse of the endless ocean before them. They knew only that they were starting.

"This is the man I will be traveling with," Dave said, introducing Shep to the crowd, many of whom he did not know himself.

"Shep and I have been dear friends from before we met," Dave said, to some ripples of laughter from the crowd. "He is one of the finest men I know and, strangely, since he doesn't like water, the only one with whom I would risk my life on an ocean voyage.

"Let's do it. Let's set sail."

"Permission to come aboard, sir," Shep called out.

Dave's dreams seemed to take on reality at that very moment.

"May your days be fair," Dave replied like the captain he was. "Welcome aboard."

Then Shep took his turn with the crowd, reading a passage from a tattered black book, "Prayers at Sea," a gift for the trip from a parishioner.

Oh, Master of the Deep, we pray for your guidance and fair passage as we set out to sea. The sea is so wide and our boat is so small. Be Thou with us. May your spirit breathe upon the sails of our hearts and lead us safely to port. Amen.

"Amen," the onlookers echoed solemnly.

A friend and his wife strummed a guitar and sang a gentle song of farewell.

Shep and Dave prepare to set sail

The song ended and unshed tears tightened the back of the men's throats and glistened in the eyes of those they loved. Sailors and spectators alike wished the speeches could go on and on -- anything to delay this parting. But, finally there was nothing more to say and the only sound was the sea lapping gently in the background. Shep's brother John L., with his usual gentle grin, snapped a few pictures. His sister Sharon, with whom his bond had been close through their young years, kissed him with tears in her eyes.

His mother, who never initiated any show of affection, also kissed him.

"I will count the days," she said.

With fear for his son still weighing heavy on his heart, John Jacob pulled Shep close and whispered in his ear, "I love you more than my life. Come home, son."

Dave's wife of twenty years, Eva, stood stoically by Mini's curved side and watched this man she loved like her own flesh set off on a journey from which he might not return. Her small arms circled both their children as if she could protect them. Hans, the eldest, the piano player whose long, slender fingers so resembled his father's, and the baby, Ben, though taller now than her by many inches, who played almost any wind instrument he could get his hands on.

Always the devoted companion, Eva would rather Dave not go, but knowing her husband's passion for the sea and for his ministry, which was somehow tied inextricably with this journey, she was unfalteringly supportive. Dave had told her he would not go if she would grieve too much for him as he crossed the ocean. He could only go with her blessing. So it was a gift she was giving him, and not in small part because of his sailing companion.

"Shep is the only man I would ever let you cross the ocean with," she had told Dave. "Your chemistry together is unique. Together, the two of you make a complete man."

It was as if she knew that what each man lacked, the other was endowed with, and that no matter how disordered each might be by himself, together they could accomplish anything.

In truth, Eva was not particularly taken with Shep, but now was compelled to give him the benefit of the doubt, despite his roughness, to intuitively care for the man she loved and return him to her doorstep. And so she let Dave go.

Eva remembered distinctly her first meeting with Shep. She and her parents had arrived one Sunday morning in 1973, at the Salvation Army's Officer Training School in the heart of San Francisco's rugged Fillmore district. Her reserved Danish family had decided to visit the school for a quick, informal tour, as Eva had announced to them only a few months before that she intended to be a candidate for officers' training school in the next session. Eva and her sister, Laurie, had been well-protected under the tutelage of their strict mother and father. The Bruhns were northwestern folks who had not been exposed to metropolitan city life before. In fact, they had not strayed far from the roof under which they lived, so though not against Eva's new vocation, they insisted on seeing the premises for themselves.

As a staff member escorted the family around the Salvation Army building, Eva glanced unobtrusively around looking for Dave Chamberlain, the handsome young man she'd met only a few months before at Spring Campaign. The tour went smoothly and Eva completed the paperwork for her return in the fall, but unfortunately had not yet seen Dave.

During their tour, the Bruhns had no doubt heard the clear voices of the cadets coming from the small gymnasium as they practiced for an upcoming spring cantata. As luck would have it, the ever-restless Shep had just excused himself from there for a drink of water, and he as bounded into the foyer, he startled the family as they were taking their leave.

Shep had never seen Eva before, but from Dave's description, this had to be her. He'd told Shep she had the cutest round cherub face and that she blushed at the drop of a hat -- which she was doing even now as Shep caught her eye.

Eva took one look at him as well, and said simply, "Shep."

"Eva," he replied.

"Have you seen Dave?" Shep asked.

Eva looked sideways at her parents, assessing their reaction to that shocking question, while rather wishing she could melt into the floorboards. She shook her head from side to side and studied her shoes.

"No…no," she mumbled, as though that was the furthest thing from her mind.

Her face must be going numb from the embarrassment, Shep thought with some amusement.

"Stay here," he commanded.

Turning on his heel, he swung nimbly around the newel post and up the stairs, bursting into the gymnasium where choir practice was breaking up.

"Guess who's downstairs!" he called to Dave. "Eva Bruhn is standing in our school right now."

Dave blanched. All of a sudden he was self-conscious. He smoothed his hair down and straightened his tie.

Well, at least I'm an almost graduate of Officers' Training School, he thought. *Surely, that will impress the family of the woman I hope to marry.*

So, years later, when Dave approached Eva about crossing the ocean and told her who his companion would be, she granted her approval. After all, Michael Shepard had been the man who had fetched Dave for her that day at the training school. Though quite too barbaric for her tastes, Shep nonetheless held a mystic place of esteem in Eva's eyes based only upon the fact that Dave considered him to be his best friend, and she loved Dave more than anyone in the world.

10

Sailing the Ocean Blue

The hugs seemed endless, the encouragement as bottomless as the ocean upon which the men would set sail. The crowd rustled with anticipation. The tears of parting were like champagne christening the little boat.

Eva stretched up and kissed Dave goodbye with Ben tucked tightly beneath her right arm and Hans unable to look up, his face buried to portside below Dave's lock-arm stance over the rail. Reaching over, Eva gently freed Hans' grip from boat and nudged him back. He dragged his arms along Mini's side with the painful reluctance of good-bye.

Shep thought to himself how fortunate Dave was to have his wife there to bid him farewell, inasmuch as his had chosen not to come at all. In fact, the day he left for San Diego from Redwood City, hauling his heavy-laden sea bag down the hallway, Shep wished that Debby would simply come to the back door and say goodbye. Instead, she called out a farewell from somewhere in the interior of the house as the door clicked shut behind him. Shep's children had cried and tugged at his pant legs, knowing they could not make the journey to see him off without their mother. Watching Dave's wife grieve genuinely for the time they would be apart, Shep envied him and felt somehow the lucky star Dave had seemingly been born under was not available to him. Though as his dearest friend, Shep found great joy in the fact that Dave had married well.

The ocean lapped restlessly nearby. The smell of Mother Sea filled the men's nostrils. They were anxious to be off. Though loved ones and friends reached up and the men reached down, touching hands and cheeks, lovingly saying farewells without words, in truth, the men had already departed. Their minds raced ahead with the surf. Already they saw themselves at the harbor's exit, heading out to open sea.

They smiled indulgently for a few more small moments accommodating the farewells, Dave steady-looking in his sea togs and custom-made sunglasses covering eyes almost blind without the built-in prescriptions; Shep in a blue-and-white striped shirt as though he were going on a resort sailing trip as a guest.

Then, as if on cue, one of the waiting shore men jumped into the pickup truck that cradled Mini and rolled the boat into the water. Mini broke loose with an almost tangible eagerness.

Though they might deny it, those left ashore felt an unspoken longing for an adventure they'd never dreamed of as they watched the two men begin to drift away. It was that yearning of which Peter Freuchen wrote in his "Book of the Seven Seas":

When gales whip the trees and rattle our windows or snow piles up outside so that no one wants to go for a walk, landlubbers snug in warm rooms are likely to tell each other how sorry they feel for all the poor sailors on a night like this.

But they feel, too, a little wistful envy of the men who brave cold and storms upon the restless water. Then on a fine day the sight of foreign seamen or of tall ships from far away or of an exotic bit of merchandise from halfway round the world or even of an oddly shaped scrap of driftwood cast up on the beach gives any of us a pang of jealousy of the men who move about over the sea viewing the wonders of the deep.

As Mini continued out of the harbor laden with her precious cargo and untold pounds of food and water, Eva's song -- the one she wrote herself -- was playing on the cassette player lashed to Mini's ledge.

My friend and my lover who holds my own heart.

My gift from the Father above is here close beside me though we're far apart.

Many waters cannot quench love.

As people cupped their mouths and yelled last greetings: "bring us a pineapple," or "go for it, you lucky sots," Mini sank gently into the water, her belly far below water line. Heavy with gear and supplies, the tiny boat's weight was way beyond her normal. In preparing for the trip, the two men had loaded one of everything imaginable aboard.

"Heck, we might as well put on a few animals," Dave had joked. "Mini is starting to resemble a miniature Noah's Ark."

Her bilge was stacked so tightly with goods that there was hardly a cubic inch of vacant space. Every corner was crammed with something: surgical equipment, oil, wood, dried food, bags of water, canned goods, tools, plastic tarps, lengths of cloth, even a small auxiliary motor with a gallon of fuel to bring the boat into the harbor at the other end of the journey. All these provisions added several hundred more pounds to Mini's riding weight. As she had slid smoothly off the trailer, the extra pounds had pushed her deep into the water. Her sides, normally rising out of the water a good two feet, balanced only six inches above sea level.

Still within sight of those wishing them well, Shep felt cool water seeping into his gleaming white sailing shoes as ocean water quickly rose to ankle-deep in the cockpit. Looking over at Dave, he noted the frozen smile on his friend's face.

"Just smile and wave," Dave ordered between clenched teeth as he continued to look stoically shoreward.

Though they knew Mini would ride low at first, the men weren't expecting the boat to immediately take on so much water. Not idly, both men wondered what would happen when the first wind arrived.

Shep's sister, Deb, not realizing the departure was so imminent, had run to the store for a roll of film. About the time Mini rounded the jetty on her way out, Deb pulled up to the dock with film in camera, only to see people walking onto the pier waving and shouting. Realizing her chance for goodbye had passed, she shamelessly begged a ride aboard a 30-foot Allegro boat named, "Phantom," which was heading Mini's way. The crew invited the remaining siblings to jump aboard, as well, to pursue the diminishing boat toward Coronado Bridge.

Oblivious to any followers and already some distance along the three-and-a-half-hour trip out of the enclosed harbor, Mini's small crew motored steadily toward open sea. As the sun stretched toward the western horizon, the Allegro began to close on Mini at mile marker seven where a clanging buoy at the ebb of the sea marked the exit from the harbor. Crowded around its base, three sea lions back-to-back, barked continuously. With bell clanging and seals barking, the Allegro came within ten meters of Mini's portside before Dave and Shep noticed the boat.

"Hey, where do you guys think you're going?" Deb grinned, shouting across the space.

With dusk gathering around them, Shep's family waved a final farewell to the little crew, then the Allegro swung sharply to port and headed back to the harbor as Mini made her way farther and farther toward Mexican waters and the dimming light gave way to darkness.

"Look," Dave said, turning to gaze back toward the San Diego skyline. For the first time on their voyage, but not the last, the two sailors could see the slightest indication of the earth's curve at the bottommost part of the silhouette. It was a sight that would become as familiar as their living room couch during the next thirty days.

As always, when Dave sailed past the harbor markings he felt so at home on the water that tears welled in his eyes. Shep, on the other hand, was scared and Dave knew it. On Shep's head was a hat emblazoned, "Chicken of the Sea."

"You have no idea how descriptive this really is," he'd joked with the crowd on shore.

Shep would always believe that Dave, upon leaving land behind that May afternoon, was an extraordinary man doing something very, very ordinary to his realm of understanding and existence, whereas Shep believed himself to be an extremely ordinary man embarking on one of the most extraordinary adventures of his life.

Wind flapped the new sail, its white dove looking almost alive and in flight. The lights of San Diego disappeared into the darkness. Simultaneously, it hit the men that this trip was no longer just some exciting talk. It was a brisk, damp evening on the Pacific Ocean and they had embarked on the manifestation of their long-imagined dream.

11

Reality Sinks In

"Well, here we are," Shep said, idly watching the canvas sails billowing away from the mast like heavy silk.

"Yep. We did it," Dave replied. "Gosh, it was great having so many people come to see us off."

"No kidding," Shep said. "It's hard to imagine, other than our families, who'd really care that two idiots are risking their lives crossing thousands of miles of sea in a sailing bathtub."

"Watch it, buddy," Dave laughed, always defensive of his little boat.

The men talked in bursts, then fell silent not knowing what else to say. The long trip on a little boat together seemed to awe the two friends into silence.

Feeling a little awkward and laughing at himself for it, Shep tugged absentmindedly at the lanyard on his coat. Dave began fiddling with the leads. It would take some getting used to, this being so close after so many years. Neither man had ever done an expeditionary trip such as this. They had both prepared somewhat by reading, "Dove," and as well, Dave had immersed himself in Captain Joshua Slocum's, "Sailing Alone

Around the World." Shep had read Thor Hyerdahl's, "Kon Tiki," and Tanya Abie's, "Maiden Voyage," but nothing could prepare them for the actual experience of spending thirty long days and nights on an expanse as vast as the Pacific Ocean.

Without realizing it precisely, their first night on this journey was almost one year to the day from that warm May evening in northern California when the two men had hatched their mighty plan to sail an ocean.

12

A Fortuitous Beginning

On May 2, of this particular year, El Nino conditions were in effect. The south bay coastals, or trade winds toward Mexico, were heavy with a phosphorescent tide, a phenomenon when algae take on an almost electric-looking light. As such, after dark on their first night out the wake showed an eerie green glow trailing back 15 or 20 feet from Mini before disappearing into the blackness.

As though enchanted, the water looked more like a fairytale liquid in some storybook than an actual ocean.

"Isn't this a nice greeting to us from the ocean?" Dave said, almost to himself. "It's rather like magic."

By its light, the men could see large creatures moving in the water near the surface.

As I watched off the stern of the boat, peering down, I see a ghost image off the stern and began to be lost in this imaginary world of the deep, Shep wrote in his ship's diary.

The two had planned this trip to be during the mildest month of the year. They anticipated no storms, bad weather, or even serious squalls. But unbeknownst to them, El Nino had other surprises in mind for their voyage.

The night air was damp and chill. By midnight, Mini was between the coast of Mexico on one side and the dark silhouette of the Mummy Islands on the other, which looked for all the world like giants laying on their backs with feet and stomachs extended. For Shep, it was the first time he'd seen an island. The first time he'd been at sea at night.

Everything was a first, he thought, including the uncomfortable feeling of such absolute remoteness from his fellow planet-dwellers.

Our isolation from family begins to sink deep into our spirits, he wrote. *The realization of where we are for some strange reason, causes each of us to cry a few tears separately and privately as the first night begins to crawl along, perhaps not as exciting as we'd imagined during the weeks prior to our departure.*

Mini's course continued south, wave by wave, the mesmerizing rhythm of water swishing by for hours. At 2 a.m., the men experienced one of he great moments of the trip.

"Hey, Shep, look at this," Dave called, bringing a sleepy Shep up from the cabin.

It was a freighter from Hong Kong heading north up the coast. Unlike cruise ships laden with lights and music and teeming with life as it sprints through the sea, this third-world freighter was a gigantic, rusty, ancient vessel, barely lit and only just lumbering along like a weary peddler with too much to carry. The freighter made no sound as its huge presence passed Mini a mile off her starboard side. The two men instinctively stood up as the monster shimmered past them, then disappeared into the darkness.

"That may be the only ship we see this side of Hawaii," Dave remarked.

13
Choosing Mini

At first, Mini had not seemed like the logical choice for an ocean-sailing vessel. Shep had what he thought was an elegant sailboat, an 18-foot Renkin called "The Zephyr," about which Dave had to let Shep down easy.

"It's just not the right craft with which to tackle an ocean, Shep," he'd said. "Trust me."

They briefly considered buying a new boat, but on minister wages that was simply not an option. As time went on, Dave began to speculate that Mini, his 20-foot dinghy, was the perfect candidate for this trip.

"I know her absolutely, Shep. I know she can do it. She has shoal-draft twin keels, meaning she can't be grounded when the tide goes out," he explained. "The boat just stands up till the tide comes back in."

What he didn't mention was that those keels could also keep her upright in stormy seas.

Dave had purchased Mini for $1,500 more than a decade before from the two men who owned her. Built more than fifteen years earlier in Portugal, Spain, Mini was a Vivacity class sloop. The men had bought her in Costa Rica, they said, and when Dave saw her tied her up at the J Street dock in Chula Vista, he fell instantly in love with the tiny sailboat.

Mini heads for open sea

"It's common knowledge in sailing circles that most people cross the ocean in boats bearing at least a $50,000 price tag," Dave had acquiesced to Shep. "Mini, on the other hand...if one romanticized her value, she's probably worth about $5,000."

"Yeah? Given her shabbiness and size, I think five hundred might be too high an estimate," Shep had joked, dodging a playful hit from Dave. "My guess is that boat should've been scuttled years ago."

"The Zephyr is fancy, Shep," Dave continued, unfazed, "but she'll cost us at least fifty days in transit. Mini can do it in thirty."

Eventually, the two men agreed that, indeed, Mini would be their vehicle of choice, and a fortuitous one as it would turn out. Small, faithful Mini had, among other virtues, a thick fiberglass hull capable of withstanding tremendously hard seas. And she was far from a factory boat.

Six months before their departure, Dave and Shep had visited a famous nautical salvage store in Newport Beach, coincidentally named "Minnie's," to look at odds and ends of sailing equipment in anticipation of retrofitting *their* Mini for the crossing. In a large wooden bin of winches, hatches and cleats, Dave pulled out a well-used, but still in good condition set of hassler gear for a self-steering vane.

Flipping over the cardboard tag attached by heavy sisal twine to the sprocket, Dave exclaimed, "No way!"

There in felt marker were the words, "from Robin Lee Graham's 'Dove'." Awestruck, the men stared at the tag.

"How did you get this?"

"Did you meet Robin Lee Graham?"

They asked the shop owner everything they could think of -- everything but the price. Whatever it was, it wasn't too high, because it was somehow magically appropriate that the Dove's equipment should end up in their hands. Like a good omen, the gear would be a talisman for their quixotic journey. With grins larger than crescent moons the two carried the Dove's n gear home like a handful of rare stardust.

In addition to installing the fated hassler, Dave made other modifications to the boat, including a custom tiller hinge built especially for Mini in a bronze foundry at Port Townsend, Washington. Retrofitted by Dave, the tiller hinge attached to a skeg rudder that he believed would be strong enough to handle the roughest of seas. He removed Mini's original mahogany rudder from the stern, which operated on a pigeon and gudgeon system, and stowed it below decks in case the new skeg should somehow be ripped from the boat. Now a backup, the old rudder rested alongside an extra inflatable dinghy with life jackets, flare guns, a water-activated emergency pulse locator (E-perb), and other vital equipment.

Always thinking, Dave tended toward being something of a mad scientist. He was always cooking up new contraptions for every application, earning him the affectionate nickname, "Dr. Gadget," from friends and family. One such contrivance was a self-steering vane he fabricated from bicycle parts.

"Look," Dave said to Shep, who seemed to be napping on a lawn chair rather than patching the fiberglass spot on Mini's side that needed fixing.

"We now have cruise control," Dave gloated. "This little baby will allow the ship's pilot to fix the boat's direction, so we can kick back and relax as the boat steers itself."

"Now, that's what I like," Shep said, appreciating getting the most function for the least amount of work.

Cutting and welding the vane pieces, Dave suddenly remembered a silly invention he'd made at school.

"Remember, Hootin' Horton?" He said to Shep, who was now at his assigned task.

Hootin' Horton had been a Toucan bird puppet Dave concocted from a litter picker and some cardboard at the training school. The crazy bird would appear suddenly from under the table at dinner to peck at unsuspecting dinner plates, or from beneath a desk to ask impertinent questions of the instructor.

"Yeah, I do," Shep said, laughing at the memory of that wacky purple and yellow critter.

"I wonder what ever happened to old Hootin' Horton," Dave wondered idly.

Dave also enlarged the water evacuation holes, or scuppers, of the cockpit so any waves coming over the boat's side could flow out as fast as possible and Mini's recovery at sea would be quick. Lastly, he filled several large, hollow spaces at the far bow end of the bilge and in and around its compartments with polystyrene foam deep enough so that, if all else failed, Mini could serve as a life raft if she were completely disabled.

"Any part of this vessel, even if she's torn in half, can stay afloat indefinitely," he told Shep with confidence.

"I can only hope you're right," Shep replied, trusting his buddy, but feeling nervous goose bumps anyway.

Just to prove his point, on the day Dave completed the auxiliary flotation, with video camera in hand, he sailed to the middle of San Diego bay, set the camera on a tripod in the middle of the cabin and removed the breach plug from the flooring. The ocean gushed in like a Yellowstone geyser from the two-inch diameter hole, flooding the boat within minutes. Dave stood in water to his knees, film still rolling. As the water flow tapered off to a mere swirl around him, he smiled widely at the camera.

"This boat is unsinkable," he gloated, giving himself an imaginary pat on the back.

As it would ultimately turn out, perhaps some

modifications Mini should have had more extensively were those dealing with communication. Originally, the men had planned to take a single sideband radio on board with which to talk back to land from the middle of ocean. However, since the entire trip was being done on the shoestring budgets of two poor clergymen, the cost of a ham radio, the time involved in licensing, and the cost of purchasing a power source to operate such equipment were all beyond the scope of anything they could adequately do. Plus, as Dave researched the possibilities, he rationalized that a radio would be nothing but a source of terror for their families. The solar capabilities for battery recharging at sea was meager and using patched-together equipment, chances were very good that the radio would go dead somewhere mid-seas.

"Just think about it, Shep," he explained. "If our families stopped getting messages from us, they'd be in agony wondering if we were alive or dead. But if they know they won't be hearing from us, they'll be able to assume we're okay."

So the two decided to make the voyage with a simple, "bon voyage," at the dock and a promised phone call when they arrived in Hilo.

Of course, the terrible downside of that decision would be that if the men perished at sea, no one would have had their last coordinates in order to search for them. No one would have any idea what had happened. Had they sunk in a storm or from a breach in the hull? Did they make a fatal miscalculation in navigation and wander lost until they ran out of food and water and vanished at sea?

If the men did not arrive in Hilo -- ever -- no one on the face of the earth would ever know what happened to them, how they had died, if indeed they had, or where their remains lay. And not just for thirty days, but forever, their loved ones would gather in kitchens, on porches, or in backyards and ponder the fate of the two men, not just what were they doing now, or where were they now, but when had they died and how?

"Do you think people would be as intrigued about us as they were about the disappearance of Amelia Earhart?" Shep joked, getting a greasy rag thrown his way in response.

"Yes, and it would be even harder to find us -- rather like trying to find Waldo somewhere in the Milky Way," Dave said.

Mini did, however, have a regular UHF CB-style radio onboard, which could reach out fourteen miles, a miniscule distance in a half-world ocean. So, for all intents and purposes, the men would be without radio communication on board until they arrived in Hawaii. Modern navigational equipment, such as a satellite navigation unit, was simply too costly. But once again, it was Dave to save the day. Ever the sailor, he had practiced celestial navigation on and off for years and was confident that somehow he could find this microscopic spot in the middle of the ocean called Hilo using the stars, sun, and moon. Tactfully ignoring Columbus's famous failure, Dave thought surely it shouldn't be too difficult. He also chose to ignore the well-known fact that celestial navigation is something of an art form as archaic as reading the entrails of a chicken in this modern day of technology. As the years go by, fewer and fewer are the men who can actually do it. Even those who can, may not always understand why exactly it works. So difficult is it that, though based completely on mathematics and trigonometric logic, some can teach classes on celestial navigation and, though understanding the process intimately, couldn't in a million moons actually accomplish the feat.

Regardless, Dave relentlessly studied the spherical trigonometry involved and committed to seeing himself and Shep from shore to distant shore with nothing more than a wristwatch and a sextant made of plastic.

"If this is a true pilgrimage, then let's do it the old way," he insisted, getting Shep's reluctant agreement.

The thoughtful Dave had even bought a second back-up sextant for Shep, whom he planned to teach this mystic art while at sea. Time would prove, however, that Shep's highly active nature was unsuited for such complicated mathematical calculations. He lost interest in the first two minutes.

"That's okay," Dave conceded graciously. "I'll do the navigation, Shep, you keep the ship's log. I hate that paperwork stuff."

Deciphering a location in this manner could take as many as two hours, depending on distractions, and had to be done twice every twenty-four hours: at 9 a.m., and at high noon, confirming the calculations with five readings each time.

Thus, day after day at sea, Shep with deep guilt at his abdication and with his brains turned to spaghetti by the motion of the ship, would *quietly* (he couldn't ignore Dave's frantic arm signaling that meant, "Don't talk, Shep, while I'm trying to do this.") watch Dave patiently pore with wrinkled brow over the calculations.

Dave calculates location with the sextant

I'll simply have to keep the navigator alive and sane, Shep thought, *rather than try and learn that bloody navigation.*

14
Sick of it Already?

S hep was seasick, and had been for the past three days. The small boat had passed by the Guadalupe Islands and was continuing south along the Mexican coast. Already both men were saturated with seawater, which never completely dried. Salt-laden, it chafed their skin and stiffened their clothing better than any boxed starch from the grocery store. As well, they found that the gallons and gallons of water they'd stored in plastic bladders as ballast in the hulls to use as drinking water, had become contaminated with the smell and flavor of gasoline from being in proximity to the spare engine gasoline containers. Though drinkable, it was unnerving. Realizing what a long time thirty days would be in this condition with putrid water, Shep weakened.

"Hey, Dave. What would you think if we turned back now?" he said, listening for the slightest hint of hesitation in Dave's reply.

"Turn back? You mean, abandon the trip and go back to port?" Dave said incredulously. "You don't really want to, do you?"

No hesitation there.

"Naw, not really," Shep said, with ill-concealed

resignation.

Experiencing another awful lurching of the gut, he imagined this must be akin to what women feel during early pregnancy and felt real sympathy for what his wife Debby had gone through.

He'd have to settle for drugs.

"Any more Dramamine?" he queried for the umpteenth time.

Dave had served as nursemaid during this, Shep's adjustment to sea life, fetching fresh water, crackers, and medication. He couldn't help wondering if indeed Shep was suited to this trip. Perhaps he should've brought one of the other guys who wanted to go -- men from his sailing club -- sailors with sea legs who were used to the sea and its ways. But the bottom line remained, there really was no other man with whom Dave would really wish to sail the ocean. Shep would figure it out soon, he hoped.

"Thanks," Shep said yet again, as he downed another Dramamine with a swig of oil-flavored water.

Shep was embarrassed by Dave's kind ministering, though grateful. Then, unbidden came the memory of a time when *he* was the nursemaid and Dave the helpless invalid. It was after the Spring Campaigns that arrived once every year during their two years of college, when every cadet went for a practical visit to an assigned church, usually during Easter season. While Dave was away for this temporary assignment he contracted the measles. Normally a plague of childhood, he was twenty and had never had them.

Upon Dave's arrival back at the citadel sporting flaming red blotches on his face and neck, the school nurse confirmed the diagnosis and demanded he be isolated from the rest of the students while the disease ran its course. Thus quarantined to an abandoned floor containing nothing more than empty rooms, closets, and stripped beds, Dave was to spend his time in the dismal Alcatraz-like confinement of a prisoner. He was to be restricted there for fourteen days, his meals ferried up to him along with his mail and school assignments, and with nothing more exciting to do but study, play his musical instruments, and have no contact with anyone at the school. Dave figured disconsolately that his most entrancing activity would likely be looking out on the mezzanine while his classmates trolled about, exercised, or cavorted while he convalesced.

As soon as Shep noticed Dave wasn't in class, and without consulting official channels for permission, he summarily skipped lunch, rolled his bedding into a huge bundle and muscled his way through the building, up the elevator and down the abandoned hall. Wedging himself through the open door, he tossed the load into Dave's barren room.

"Here I am, buddy ol' pal," he announced. "I'm here to spend the next two weeks with you until you're good as new."

Having gone through measles as a child, Shep had a natural immunity.

He didn't say anything, but gratitude and relief covered Dave's face as thickly as the red splotches.

Amounting to a highly brash move in a restricted school such as this, Shep was forthwith summoned to the chief officer's office.

"Ahem..." the CO began uncomfortably. Fully aware that the school was located in the heart of San Francisco, he simply had to ask: "Is it possible, er...are you and Dave *homosexuals*?" he stuttered out.

"What?!" Shep retorted, surprised. "You've got to be kidding!"

Relief spread across the chief officer's face, which was almost as red as Dave's, when Shep assured him that he and Dave were simply friends.

Shep could hardly wait to get back upstairs and report to Dave that administration thought maybe he and Dave were gay.

Many years later, that question still had the power to make the two laugh hysterically.

Two weeks sped by as Shep alternated between his schoolwork and carrying for his invalid friend. It was like an adventure to him.

On not a few evenings, Shep would wrap a bandana around his head like the thief he was, and sneak down to the mammoth refrigerator in the mess hall to liberate Frosty Pops, knowing their great medicinal value for the feverish Dave. He imagined himself as something like a Zorro on his nightly, albeit, righteous raids.

Strangely enough, measles were not the only thing Dave caught that spring. He was also bitten by the infamous love bug and it would not be long before Shep would lose the lion's share of David Chamberlain's attention, not to a disease, but to a girl.

15
Deck Duties

On day four at sea, Shep's sea legs came out from hiding and his nausea receded. Feeling as though this whole gig might not be so bad after all, he joined Dave in organizing their life at sea.

Captain Dave insisted there be an orderly routine, not only to keep Mini shipshape, but to keep the men on an even keel, metaphorically speaking.

"Busy hands are happy hands," he chortled.

His first healthy day at sea was like a miraculous vacation for Shep, free of duties or regularities, but by the first watch at sundown, Captain Dave had established a routine he expected them to stick to as fastidiously as would the Royal Navy. First, the two chaplains would begin the day with prayer, he said, then send the sun to bed with an evening one. In between, Dave ran the ship as if the two were a crew of six. Each had assigned tasks.

"Would it help if I complained to the boss?" Shep whined, noting with disappointment there was no sympathy in his shipmate's austere gaze.

Mini's tiny cabin was six feet wide and five feet high. The two Plexiglas windows were covered with rust-colored, burlap-like curtains. The windows needed the gray sea film washed off every other day. The two padded and upholstered berths on either side of the 18-inch alley had to be thumped and straightened. The blankets, life preservers and duffle bags filling Mini's small front V-berth had to stay organized. Food supplies, matches, books, toilet paper, teapot, and clothing had to always be re-stowed in the three shallow hatches and their polyurethaned plywood doors latched tightly.

Mini's Spartan "kitchen" sported a built-in ice chest in the right berth. A 10-inch gimbaled silver "stove," sat beneath their only vanity item: a wood-framed oval mirror above a small wooden shelf. To the left hung an oven Dave had fabricated from an old fire extinguisher. It had a square hole cut in its face and a 3-inch steel pipe (soon rusty) ran through the ceiling for ventilation. Below that was a drop-in brass bucket overhung with a brass pump faucet. Spanning the kitchen accouterments, humble as they were, was a 15-inch green Formica drop-in counter that bridged the berths and had to be wiped down and kept tidy as well. On either side of the hatch opening, like small inefficient sconces from a third-rate hotel, were two wooden cupboards with thumb latches that held more supplies: dishes, mugs, packets of Cream of Wheat, a flashlight, notebooks, and Mini's license. Taped to the front were photos of Dave, Eva, Hans and Ben; Shep, Debby, Jake and Mandy, and one of Mini herself. To the right of the hatch door was their one concession to communication: the 6-inch white Zephyr radio with its push-button microphone.

Under the hatch was another two-and-a-half-foot storage space with yet more storage items, including a five-gallon utility bucket that served as the men's toilet. When nature called, they'd haul it onto deck, hang it over the side and scoop in five inches of seawater, do their business, then dump its contents into the great reservoir of the sea.

"This is no frills living," Dave joked, "but it's home."

The only thing Mini lacked was what a woman wouldn't have gone to sea without: a sign nailed above the door that read, "Home Sweet Home."

Deck watches began promptly at 8 p.m. Before then, the men would make some supper, though the two found they were seldom hungry at sea, not from seasickness, but boredom. They seemed to have lost their appetites upon leaving the dock. Maybe it had something to do with watching their loved ones and land recede into the distance with only the unknown to ponder and many days ahead stretching in front of the hull. Even days and days after leaving the dock, they would still feel that way. Of course, it might also have had to do with their lack of gastronomic enthusiasm for MREs, or, "Meals Ready to Eat," that they'd purchased at a military surplus store. The MREs were silver foil-wrapped packets of stew or pasta, enchiladas or steaks. The one thing they had in common was very little flavor.

"Do these all taste like boiled-into-submission cardboard?" Shep lamented.

"Well, the beef's not too bad, but this chicken -- it *stinks*!" Dave concurred.

"Yeah. I don't care what the contents say, there is no way these can possibly contain real, honest-to-goodness, edible, authentic food," Shep said.

Though they stayed active hoisting and folding sails and swimming daily, the men simply couldn't work up an appetite. Like some marooned sailors on a forgotten island, many was the day Shep and Dave would relax in the sunshine and make laborious verbal lists of all the luscious fare they'd eat when they hit shore.

"Soft-serve ice cream," Shep would blurt out.

"Not so," Dave would come back. "It's Baskin Robbins' 31 flavors for me!"

The list would go on and on.

Steak. Lobster. Mashed potatoes. Garden tomatoes. Homemade sourdough bread. Peas. Fresh milk. Clean water!

It didn't help their appetites or outlook that the gallons and gallons of water they'd meticulously stored in plastic bags in Mini's open hulls tasted like gasoline. It wouldn't kill them, but neither was it pleasant drinking.

"I had a desalinization kit I'd been working on before we left," moaned the always-prepared Dave. "But it was one precaution I didn't think we'd actually need."

"No sweat," Shep replied. "You did bring something even more important -- the latrine!"

It was true. Their bathroom facility was something Dave had been more than prescient about. Boat latrines are infamous for malfunctioning. It was exactly that which had become the bane of a now-famous young mariner, Tania Abie, who at eighteen had successfully traveled 27,000 miles across multiple oceans entirely alone but for the company of her cat. Indeed, her latrine had given Abie nothing but grief and difficulty for most of her two-and-a-half-year journey upon the oceans of the world.

Perhaps it was recalling Abie's experience, or maybe just inspiration, but one night before the Crossing, Dave had a dream that there was something wrong with Mini's latrine. She still had the original one that had been installed when she was built in Portugal, a small porcelain contraption set in a wood frame positioned in her hull. Upon waking the next day, Dave went immediately to Mini's toilet, grasp it at the edges and pulled gently. The rotted timbers gave way with a sickening crunch, leaving the gleaming bowl in his hands. Rather than replace it and risk any problems on the journey, Dave chose simplicity. The men would use a five-gallon bucket with a toilet seat rigged atop. Nothing could go wrong there. Well, almost nothing. That decided, he patched and fiberglassed over the hole in Mini's hull where the latrine had been. The only drawback to the bucket turned out to be some slight pinching of the private areas if one were not careful in mounting or dismounting the makeshift toilet.

Other grooming rituals were simple aboard ship, as well. To brush their teeth, the men could use either the tainted drinking water, or more preferably, salt water directly from the ocean, which proved to be healthy for their gums anyway.

In fact, most things aboard ship were uncomplicated and in good weather, "the livin' was easy," as Dave liked to say.

In the evenings before first watch, the two would sit outside in the cockpit with a deck of cards playing hand after hand of Gin Rummy. If any ocean life had been listening, it would have heard the pitter-patter of playing cards being shuffled and reshuffled together, then echoing with a slap, slap, slap, as one or the other dealt the hand.

"Wait a minute," Dave would say, if Shep won too often. "Did you just cheat, my card shark friend?"

"Absolutely not, my preacher buddy," Shep would

laugh. "I'm just psychic about these things…or lucky sometimes."

Winning, losing, winning, losing, laughing, talking, Dave and Shep only rarely concentrated on the cards themselves. The images on the cards were but a temporary distraction from duty or relaxation.

"Another hand?" became the inevitable question.

"Yes?"

"Yes."

Until, finally it was time for the first watch, which was always Shep's. At eight o'clock sharp, Dave would head down below adjusting his harness and getting comfortable, while the two chatted through the open gangway as Shep manned the helm and Dave made ready for sleep.

16
Harnessing Up

Each man wore a nylon web harness that crisscrossed atop their clothing. Culminating with a snap-ring of steel in the middle of their chest, it was hooked to a rope that could be easily attached to or detached from a cleat anchored into the floor of the cockpit. This assured that a man on deck, if washed overboard, would remain tethered to the boat in the hopes he could pull himself up the side, or at least hail the other partner rather than disappearing unseen into the sea. Shep and Dave wore their harnesses faithfully both day and night no matter their position on the ship's exterior.

Another safety precaution they took was having an athletic whistle such as a referee or coach might use, that they each wore around their neck. Like the harness, it was not to be removed at any time. If washed overboard and unable to yell loud enough to rouse the other man, the shrill sound of the whistle would surely awaken the sleeping shipmate.

That first night, as Dave unsnapped his harness and headed below, he turned back from the gangway, placed his arms atop the doghouse and said, "Whatever happens, Shep, remember -- you never, *ever* unhook that harness. Not even if it's uncomfortable. Not even for a second. Because if I come back up here two hours from now and you're not on this boat, it won't ruin my big trip, my big vacation…it will ruin my entire life and nothing will ever be the same."

Shep harnessed up

"I promise," Shep said solemnly. "If I'm out here and you're sleeping, whatever else is not connected, my harness will be."

Especially during the storm that was even now sneaking up behind them, when swinging on whipping shrouds or retrieving ropes to their pulleys, their harnesses were crucial.

This isn't bad at all, Shep thought, as he manned his first watch.

The two hours passed rather nicely except for the dull pain he felt trying to stay awake. The lulling rhythm of the waves' chop against the bow and the roll of the ocean sliding past beneath the gunnels could hypnotize a man in minutes. Though Shep had pledged to keep watch to the horizon at all times and be alert, he often caught his head dipping down toward his chest before jerking back up to stare intently forward with eyes wide. In the dark of night at the helm, the only visible light came from the tiny safety light atop the 28-foot mast, which emitted a dim glow that shone upward onto the sails creating a ghost-like image above his head.

As well, forward in the cockpit was a fully gimbaled marine compass that balanced in an orb of liquid light. As the directional rosette floated freely back and forth, it pointed the direction of the ship as it listed easily port to starboard, port to starboard. The motion of the illuminated compass was the only other light the pilot could see while sitting at the helm. Indispensable, the compass allowed the helmsman to maneuver the ship through the night if hand steering became necessary. Shep found that the slow movement of this luminous sphere five feet from his eyes also mesmerized him toward sleep as surely as a hypnotist's swinging watch fob.

The nights were cold and damp with ocean spray and breeze and only the sheen of the water for comfort in the pitch-black night. Below in the cabin a man could gather some warmth and comfort, but in the exposed cockpit it was elusive. More often than not, whoever was navigating would wear a knit stocking cap with jacket hood up and strings tied beneath his neck, gloves and boots snugged on, and foul weather gear tightened.

Dave on watch in foul weather gear and harness

The aptly named foul weather gear lived up to its name on occasion when a man, urinating off the deck in bad weather, would miss the ocean and instead soak the felt lining of his bib overalls, thus creating truly foul weather gear.

His watch concluded at five minutes to ten every night, whereupon Shep would tap gently on the cabin door.

"Your watch is coming up, skipper," he'd intone, on which cue, Dave would roll to an upright position, slide into his boots, pull on his heavy watch coat and step up out of the cabin. With hands still warm from sleep, he'd grab the cold steel shackle and clip himself in. Shep would then unclick his shackle -- which he jokingly referred to as leg irons -- and gratefully retire to the cabin.

One night Dave was sleeping so soundly that he lost his bearings. When Shep called down for the next watch, Dave didn't respond. Grasping the top of the hatch, Shep dropped the two-and-a-half feet down into the gangway, startling Dave awake.

Disoriented, a big smile lighting his face, Dave said, "Shep! What are you doing here?!" as if it were the biggest, but most pleasant surprise in the world. Dreams being as dreams are, it fled so fast Dave couldn't even tell Shep where he'd been.

Conversely, at five to midnight, Dave's deep voice would call down, "Brother Shep, come out of there. Rise up and walk."

Shep would call sleepily back, "I'm coming," rubbing the rough stubble on his face to shake off the sleep. Still clad in coat and boots from the last watch, Shep would make his way up top. Again, the ceremonial clasping and unclasping of the shackles would mark another two-hours' passage. As sure as clockwork, this changing of the watch went on through all the long nights of the crossing.

17

Magic at Sea

Strange things can happen at sea in the darkness, as Shep soon found out on a first watch. It was getting a bit late on one particular May evening. Things were as calm on the water as a sleeping babe. White foamy spindrift floating gently by, together with the motion of the boat, had lulled Shep into a light sleep. As smoothly as Fred Astaire and Ginger Rogers executing a twirl, Mini whirled backwards 180 degrees and began sailing backwards. Sensing a change, Shep jolted awake to find the sea bubbles over the side of the boat passing by backwards. Because the seas were calm, the sails had locked in sideways.

"It was like being in a twilight zone movie," he told Dave the next morning. "Like lucid dreaming."

Releasing the jack lines and adjusting the boom and sails, it took Shep forty minutes to straighten it all out and get moving forward.

Dave had his own memorable watch. One night he sat at the tiller in darkness as complete as a pot with the lid on. The seas were so glossy smooth that they reflected the stars as clearly in the water as if they were in the heavens and not merely echoing their pinpoint light beneath on the sea.

"I felt like I was on Disney's Peter Pan boat ride through the night skies," he told Shep. "It was the most magical moment of my life."

The best call of the day for Shep was when his end-watch came at 6 a.m. By then, the sun was on the horizon and the smooth sea dazzled like a bright green emerald. Animated by the light, it was another night down and on to a new day.

This newly dawn hour was a wonderful time for both men. For one thing, it meant a steaming cup of coffee, courtesy of Shep. Before calling Dave up, he'd fill the alcohol-burning stove, set a match to it and put some water to boil.

The little you can give to each other at sea is muted in many ways, Shep thought, *but there is no mistaking the charity of a good cup of coffee on any given morning.*

That routine allowed Dave to wake slowly and relish not being aroused abruptly. He knew the helm was secure, the sails trimmed, and that Mini was making good headway. Inevitably, he would sit up and grab a musical instrument, most often his small metal flute, play a tune, then read aloud a chapter from an ongoing book while the coffee brewed.

Breakfast was a shared responsibility. Whoever's turn it was would fry an egg, often together with a grated potato, splash on some ketchup and toss on some canned fruit for the sake of cuisine and health. But each had their favorite meals. Dave's specialty was a soup that Shep loved, filled with carrots and spuds; and Shep in turn made authentic French fries for Dave's fast food fix.

Each man had a metal plate, a set of utensils and a cup, all of which they washed daily, trading shifts on that chore. Into a five-gallon bucket went the dishes. Holding the bucket over the side, they'd soap and rinse the dishes with their hands, then set them tidily aside for the next meal.

One of the small tragedies of the trip occurred on Shep's turn at this duty. Dave had provided Mini with a gleaming brass pot for washing dishes, hands or clothes, which the men used daily for any number of tasks. It was a treasure of construction with etchings of exotic patterns on its side and double handles for gripping. Its lustrous gold color complemented Mini's décor of hunter green upholstery edged in maroon, as well as the rich mahogany wood trim and brass fittings of her cabin. It so happened that Dave was inordinately proud of this brass basin and considered it more than a simple bucket. He thought of it as a symbolic laver, like the ones in the Old Testament that priests placed in the courtyard for spiritual foot washings and bathing ceremonies.

On this particular morning, Shep washed the dishes, rinsed and set them aside, then swung the heavy basin out to the side of the ship to toss out the water. Losing his grip on the slippery pot, it flew into the ocean along with the soapy water.

"Dave!" Shep called in dismay.

Appearing at his side, Dave watched sadly as the lovely pot caught the sunshine as if clad in real gold as it sank swiftly to the bottom -- another treasure for Davy Jones' infamous locker.

"Oh, Dave. I'm so sorry," Shep said, breaking the stunned silence, but knowing that anything he said would be inadequate.

He knew Dave was not only devastated, but also probably very angry. For all his usual equanimity, Dave did exhibit an occasionally fiery fit of temper, something he usually suspended when it came to Shep.

Years ago at officer's school, when they were playing basketball one day, Shep remembered that temper in action. Messing around as usual, not being the dedicated sportsman Dave was, Shep began flinging a rough hemp rope from side to side. It accidentally thrashed upwards at the exact moment Dave turned to make a tricky basket shot and hit him in the face. He whirled around in a flash, so angry his face was iridescent, his eyes a flashing light show. An angry red flush extended to the tips of his ears. Shep's bravado wilted as he saw the rage on his friend's face. But as Dave registered just who it was who'd stung him with the rope, his fury drained as fast as it had come. Shep had no illusions that there was no other man alive who would receive such mercy from Dave.

Now, as the cherished laver sank from sight, Shep knew once again that only he could have gotten away with such a travesty.

As the incident lost its poignancy, Dave was as gracious as ever.

"Well, you never know. Maybe some future deep-sea treasure hunter will come upon that basin and think maybe it was lost from the deck of some ancient ship from Babylonia, Assyria, or Persia," he joked.

⚓

After coffee and kitchen duty, cabin cleanup was the next order of the day, which meant swabbing the decks most days, not that they were really dirty, but more to satisfy the necessity for routine, Shep secretly thought.

It was important to keep Mini in tip-top shape, so the men also patched any leaks, greased squeaks, and made any other small necessary repairs. Then, mid-to-late morning they'd hang about and spend some time dreaming of Hawaii, talking, or entertaining each other after often long and arduous rehearsals.

One morning as Dave sat relaxing at the rudder, up came an alien from the cabin. Shep had dragged out an aluminum survival blanket from the gear box, wrapped it around himself, then set a matching aluminum cooking pot on his head, looking very much like a shiny mummy from outer space.

"What do you think, Dave? It's my new solar outfit. Should keep me warm as toast in this breeze."

The two laughed, holding their sides, as the tears streamed down their cheeks.

It was part of what Dave loved about Shep -- that wacky sense of humor. Born years too late, Dave always regretted that he'd missed the golden age of vaudeville. So the little skits Shep came up with were both touching and hilarious to him.

On another lazy afternoon, Shep sashayed up the gangway with a shirt wrapped pirate-style around his head, an eye-patch cobbled together from black electrical tape and a hand-painted tattoo inked on one bicep.

But perhaps the best was the stovepipe hat. One of the modifications Dave had made to Mini was adding a makeshift stove in the middle of one of the two side bunks in the cabin. It was of heavy metal and gimbaled on the bottom so as to rock with the boat and not upset the soup, or whatever was simmering within the pot sitting on its plate. The stove was heated from the bottom with a Sterno candle. Swinging stoves are nothing new to ocean-going ships, but certainly this miniature creation was one-of-a-kind, thanks to Dave's ability to forage for odds and ends and cobble them together.

Perhaps I've missed my calling, he thought, standing back as the metal cooled on the stove's creation day. *Maybe I should have become an inventor after all.*

But quite early in the journey, sadly, the men found the stove didn't work well. It heated too slowly and any smoke or steam generated from the food floated through the cabin like the swirling mist from Aladdin's magic lamp, choking them into fleeing outside. So finding it useless, but entertaining, Shep finally disassembled the unit and, turning it upside down, found that the rocker arm for the gimbaled portion made a dandy chin strap and the pot portion fit his round head quite nicely.

With panpipes dangling off his side like Peter Pan, yellow rubber gloves on his hands and a spyglass held to his eye, Shep quite resembled some strange futuristic sailor from Dr. Nemo's Nautilus. Best of all, the outfit got a good laugh from Dave.

The aforementioned panpipes were used for music as well as costume décor. There were two other musical instruments on board, too: Shep's small stringed guitar that looked more a large ukulele, and Dave's Ten-penny Irish "tin" whistle, which was nothing more than a primitive flute. Twelve-inches long and pierced with a half-dozen holes, the tin whistle was a little crooked, but

when blown, emitted a delicate, faraway sound that could have been made by a forest nymph fingering the flute in an emerald corner of the Land o' the Green.

Dave didn't know why he had such a fascination with wind-blown instruments, but he'd taken to the trombone as a fish to water, though he also loved flutes and recorders and such. At home, he had a harsh-sounding 1877 ten-hole ceramic Ocarina, which he loved. But then, Dave loved all fipple-vessel flutes for some reason.

When I get back home, he thought to himself, *I'll invent a mouthpiece, one that could turn an ocarina into a trumpet, or a tuba, or a French horn. I must remember that.*

He was thinking, too, how loose his lips would get on this trip. Musicians know that a trombone player has to play everyday to keep his lips 'in shape.'

Too bad I didn't think to invent that mouthpiece before this trip so I could practice, he mused. *Heaven knows there wasn't room to bring my trombone.*

Besides, he chuckled aloud, *hearing a trombone in the middle of the ocean every day might have driven my shipmate mad!*

Although the two collaborated on several musical pieces together on the trip, there was one special song they'd committed to play on this voyage. Neither men knew its real name, but they knew most people their age on the planet could automatically recite the lyrics. From the old cartoon of the spinach-eating sailor, it was "Popeye, the Sailor Man." But try as they might, the two could never quite nail it. Making miscues and mistakes, the two inevitably ended up groaning with frustration before trying again, then again. Slower, then slower, note-by-note they labored on until they would inevitably reach that one impossible passage.

"Even Popeye himself could probably never play this," Dave groaned.

"Well, we don't have any spinach aboard. What do you expect?" Shep replied.

But there was one song they had down pat. Shep on his guitar and Dave on his flute would put the sun to bed every night with a duet of, "Danny Boy," its strains so lovely across the empty ocean it could make a whale cry.

"Even though we're only entertaining fish now, remember when we made those banjos, Shep?" Dave said one night, leaning back on the aft cabin wall as the song ended.

"Sure," Shep grinned, "But I don't know that the sidewalk strollers of San Francisco enjoyed our music any more than the fish do."

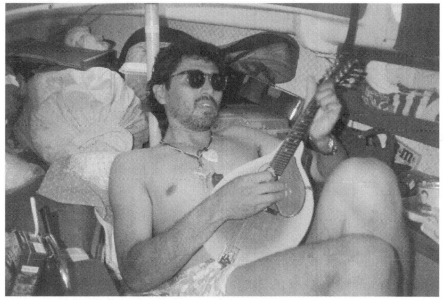

Shep strumming his mandolin aboard ship

It had been yet another season at officer's training school when Dave and Shep decided to make musical instruments, mostly five-string primitive fretless banjos, for which they fashioned hoops from the shop's scrap wood. The boys bought thin rawhide skins from a downtown drum shop to cover the faces and made operable friction pegs on the heads of necks, which they hand-carved themselves. With various gauges of hard nylon deep-sea fishing line, they had managed to produce instruments that actually worked. On warm summer evenings the boys would take their makeshift instruments, sit on the school's front stoop and play ballads. One of the hits on the radio at the time was "Dueling Banjos," and Dave and Shep could stop people dead in their tracks with just the opening few notes of that piece, much to the amusement of their colleagues.

"You guys crack me up," hollered Bob Wells, hanging out his window on the second story. "I can't believe you're out there torturing the public with your screeching again."

"Watch it," Dave hollered back, "or we'll sneak into your room at midnight and play the William Tell Overture!"

Neither of the boys had played banjo before, but both were innately musical. Dave could play almost any brass wind instrument in existence, though the trombone was his particular area of expertise, and Shep had strummed guitar ever since he saw the Beatles on the Ed Sullivan show and decided to be just like them. As the two became more proficient in banjo playing, they each chose a strumming specialty.

Dave began studying books on traditional Appalachian playing, and especially took to the claw hammer method. Shep preferred to do straight-pluck Bluegrass fingerpicking. Either way, with banjo heads taut and tuned, the two could make plenty of noise between them, not unlike their musical prowess on Mini.

"Remember when we had to ask Chris Marsh for money to buy banjo supplies?" Shep asked.

Chris March had been the financial officer on the training school staff, a recent graduate who'd been reappointed to the school. A free spirit, Chris was at home in the '60s, her auburn-blonde hair styled in an Afro straight off the stage of "Godspell." She'd converted denim overalls into a skirt and embroidered it with fanciful Hippie peace signs, daisies, crosses and a Christian fish.

All the boys seemed to have a crush on the beautiful Chris, mooning at her unguardedly as she strummed her bohemian guitar covered with rainbow stickers and strapped on with macramé. But of all the love-struck students, Chris singled out only one: Dave Chamberlain.

"So, you never really told me what happened at your 'private' dinner with Chris, Dave," Shep prodded, remembering how Chris had invited Dave upstairs to her apartment where he unexpectedly found flickering candles and homemade food steaming on the table.

"All the rest of us poor schmucks were waiting in our dorm rooms in agony, imaging what was going on up there," Shep sighed.

Even all these years later, Dave still blushed to think of it.

"Well, there I was like a lamb to the slaughter," he joked, then turned serious. "I didn't know what to think. I suddenly realized she had romantic intentions toward me. I really hadn't guessed."

Though flattered, Dave felt only brotherly love for Chris. He was saving his heart for a certain little Danish girl he'd met recently.

"So nothing happened. Well, I suppose it was just as well," Shep sighed.

Banjos or no banjos, Dave and Shep had always played music together. Dave could play almost any tune professionally and Shep knew the popular music of the day, both secular and religious. Though not the polished musician Dave was -- Shep had struggled to take music lessons, buying them with his paper route money -- he'd learned to play some instruments moderately well by ear: guitar, piano, mandolin…though he'd never learned to read music.

Several times when they were short of cash, the two would hop a streetcar at Fisherman's Wharf with instrument cases in hand and place themselves strategically by the cannery, an idea in no way original: they'd seen other musicians doing so with cases propped open for any passing tips. Shep would need only to name a tune and key and Dave would float the trombone notes through the night air as tourists passed by. It wasn't hard to see that the boys were enjoying themselves every bit as much as anyone kind enough to pause and listen were, whether it was a group of sailors waxing homesick to the boys' sentimental ballad about, "the girl left behind," or tourists enjoying, "I Left My Heart in San Francisco."

Reclining on Mini's cockpit benches now with guitar and flute in hand, the two were lost in thought.

"We should've taken these to Kubachev," Dave said, referring to his and Shep's 1989 trip to the Soviet Union. Dave had asked Shep to join him and a band of six other musical youths -- "non-denominational Charismaniacs" as Shep later jokingly referred to them.

A Calvary Chapel pastor had organized the expedition at the request of a Russian group interested in Christianity. With Professor of Religion permission slips from the Russian government tucked into their passports, the band, "Second Childhood," went as minstrels to minister to the people -- the first musical Christian group allowed into Russia for decades. Three weeks before, the coup, they played in the largest opera house in the city to an overflow crowd.

The group not only brought music, they smuggled in a thousand small Bibles -- books not yet legal in the country. One Bible was worth two month's wages on the Black Market, though the band passed them out for free-- secretly, of course.

Shep had taken his rare baby blue Adamis guitar made of graphite to Russia. When he met a Latvian there who was playing like an angel on one of the most inferior guitars he'd ever seen, Shep gave him the guitar.

I can always get another one, he'd thought. *But this poor man will never be able to have a guitar worthy of his skill.*

18

Bring in the Clowns

After a lunch of unexciting MRE fare, the men's afternoons included reading, clowning, and rigging, not necessarily in that order. As the daily tedium took its toll, playful Shep would inevitably dig into the supplies and dress up once again, trying to make Dave laugh. One of Dave's favorite pranks was the story of the dorky and incompetent First Mate that Shep made up one afternoon and would retell at random when the two needed a good laugh.

It seemed the wacky First Mate always had the best of intentions, but his every plan would invariably go awry. One scenario Shep enacted was when First Mate tried to improve the conditions aboard by cutting the rigging into delicate strips for dental floss so the sailors could maintain good dental hygiene. Others were when First Mate used the sails to make the sailors matching regatta shirts, or threw the ship supplies off the stern to keep the sharks preoccupied. If all else failed, First Mate would simply open the latch to the fuse box, reach inside, say to the skipper, "I think I've found the problem," then convulse as if electrocuted and fall to the floor. First Mate steadfastly refused to revive until Dave was convulsing as well, but with laughter.

Then there was the saga of David and Goliath. Shep created an enactment from the famous Bible story especially for Dave, as David was the obvious hero of this tale.

Shep rigged a sling of sorts with some parachute cord he'd found in a provision bag, tying it to the corners of some heavy oilcloth he'd also uncovered below. Peeling down to the skin, he wrapped his proverbial loins in a towel representing the animal skin the Biblical David would have worn, and tied a rag around his forehead. With its ends dangling in front of his left ear, Shep thought he looked quite the hero part.

Rising from the gangway into the sunlight above, he caught Dave's attention at the tiller without much effort.

"Behold, the emissary of God!" he announced. "I shall thus slay the enemy of our people -- the giant and indestructible Goliath -- with my tiny little slingshot. Yes. I'm a very good shot."

Shep then prepared his weapon, loading a nut stolen from some extra fix-it parts stored below. Aiming far out to sea, he challenged his opponent.

"Come forth, you big bully. I shall herewith slay your meanness with a single shot!"

With that, Shep raised his arm above his head as would a mighty soldier, bent backwards and began spinning the sling around his head faster and faster, preparing to let the nut fly – and thunked himself on the forehead, then made a faux fall overboard into the ocean.

He came up spluttering and laughing, pleased to note that his own hero, Dave, was doubled up laughing in his high and dry position in the cockpit.

It was exactly this magnetism and creativity that

made Shep unique. His sister Sharon, six years his junior, was one of his favorite playmates as a child.

"His creative mind never stopped," she was fond of saying. "I really felt I grew up in the shadow of a very unusual person. He wasn't like other little kids. If most kids were making biscuits, Shep would make croissants."

And he sewed.

"He'd bring out Mom's sewing machine and say, 'I'll make clothes for your Barbie doll,'" Sharon would recall with a giggle. Or at the grocery store, Shep would tell her to "pick the best box." Once home, they'd build something magnificent and fun from the cardboard, like an airplane or a castle.

One time, Shep found a small bird that had fallen from the power lines because of electrocution, old age or heart attack, he knew not. Shep plucked it thoroughly, cleaned it, then basted and baked it as if it were a 13-pound turkey. His friends were entranced.

This ability of his to take the ever mundane and create something marvelous and entertaining came in extremely handy during the doldrums of the ocean crossing.

After Dave handed Shep back into the boat, they took turns loading spare nuts, or bolts, or food scraps…whatever they had at hand, and lobbing them extreme distances from the boat with the homemade sling.

"Now, *that* was some fun," Dave sighed, as they relaxed later, stretched lazily out on the cockpit benches.

⚓

Dinner always took the men straight into evening with a steaming cup of tea from Dave's silver teapot with the wooden handle, which he poured with great ceremony a la pinky finger extended. Though seemingly superfluous, he had refused not to bring it.

"You're a descendent of Lord Chamberlain: Grand Admiral of the Sea for the British throne, aren't you, my snooty friend?" Shep would joke.

Of course, Lord Chamberlain: Grand Admiral of the Sea wasn't a documented real person, but Dave got a kick out of the inference anyway.

Finally, the opening of the box of playing cards signaled the certain end to another day and the beginning of another endless night watch. By those benchmarks, the friends traveled the hundreds upon hundreds of miles in relative contentment.

19

Doldrums Reflections

It's a given that any trip on an immense and seemingly endless ocean can take on a bland sameness as day after day the blue-green water passes beneath the bow and another sun rises and sets, so the men determined to create rituals to mark the time.

At the time of the launching, somebody with a Polaroid camera had taken photos of Dave and Shep standing in the rigging arm-in-arm, cheek-to-cheek and wearing their best smiles. The shutter clicked, the film surged forward. Within a minute, a half-dozen almost identical poses had developed in their hands. It would be these photographs that would later connect the two with all that was not ocean.

In what some sailors call the "shrine," aka the lazaret -- a waterproof compartment in the stern usually containing spare rope, flashlights, and other emergency odds and ends -- the two had stored a small liquor supply of mini wine bottles, which sparkling liquid they reserved for certain special events. Every two hundred miles, after drinking the contents of a bottle, Dave and Shep would write a simple message, cork it into the bottle and send it splashing into the sea.

They took turns writing the spare messages:

Hello from (longitude) and (latitude). We're Dave and Shep. We're crossing the Pacific Ocean from California to Hawaii on a 20-foot boat. If you find this on any particular day of any year in any location around the world, please contact us. Fair weather and good winds from the California sailing ship Mini.

With each small message they included their home addresses and phone numbers.

Carefully hand-rolling the note inside one of the Polaroid snapshots, they'd shove it down the neck of the pint-size wine bottle and hurl it off Mini's stern into the frothing wake, then stand at attention, their hands touching their foreheads in silent salute, and watch for long minutes as the bottle began to drift away on the powerful currents to parts unknown.

"Do you think anyone will really find these?" Dave said.

"It's possible," Shep replied, thinking that when and if their bottles washed up on some foreign soil that some hands beyond their own would uncork their message and read of their voyage. After all, didn't bottles, baubles and glass net balls, purposely or accidentally set adrift, easily spend seven to ten years afloat following currents to remote beaches on every continent on the planet? Anywhere, in fact, that the endless ocean touches land? Why, even now somewhere someone's ankles were touching the sea that they were so far abroad upon. Surely, there was a remote chance that at the ocean's edge, maybe someday someone somewhere might find one of these water-cast bottles and just for the thrill of doing so, contact the erstwhile sailors named within.

And so it went: another two hundred miles; another bottle into the sea, and so on for the entire voyage. With the casting of each message, the men's minds would drift with the bottle, not to parts unknown, but to their own homes in California, on solid terra firma. What were their wives doing now, they wondered: Washing? Cleaning? Singing? Sleeping? And their children…were they at school at that moment learning the rudiments of music theory or mathematics, or were they having a rousing game of softball or playing Mario Brothers video games?

Dave thought of his first-born, Hans, now eleven -- slender as a reed and as talented at music as his father. What was he doing now? Then there was dear sweet seven-year-old Ben, with his father's wry sense of humor. Was he getting his homework done? Little did Dave know then that Ben would have his future in the Coast Guard, perhaps in part because the family sailing trips to Catalina every year at Christmas had fired his love of the ocean.

Shep's eldest was twelve-year-old Amanda Lynn. Said together it sounded like "mandolin," one of Shep's favorite musical instruments. On her eighteenth birthday, Shep intended to give her his own mandolin, a beautiful blue-iridescent one that sang like a rare bird. Mandy was smart and beautiful, good in school and dutiful, as an eldest often is.

Little John, who'd turn ten while Shep was at sea, would surely be skateboarding the sidewalks with his buddies, or stopping for fries and a coke at In-and-Out Burger, a smile lighting his good-natured face.

Having no communication with land from on board was both a blessing and a curse. Though it gave the men no chance to actually ring up their loved ones to check in, leave a message of love or catch up on news, it also meant they could remember them with all the love and fondness distance can create.

So while Dave wondered if Eva was doing all right, not fretting overly at his absence or worrying about any sea straits he might or might not be in, Shep wondered if Debby even thought of him, and if so, what would those thoughts be? He wondered how things could've gotten so bad between them. Thinking back to their early courting days when he had a ministry in San Diego and Debby was stationed in the Mission District's outreach center in San Francisco, he remembered them driving all the miles in-between to spend weekends together, having picnics and walking the beach. He remembered how beautiful he thought she was with that sprig of freckles across her nose; her red hair lit by the sun. It all seemed so simple and perfect then.

Shep knew his selfish ambition contributed to their problems. Both his strength and his weakness -- his drive -- had perhaps eclipsed his love and concern for her. He'd forgotten to count the cost of his insatiable hunger to climb upward in the organization. A dynamic leader, Shep was a powerful speaker. Debby was the support system, the person who kept the records and did the paperwork that oiled the machine and made their efforts complete. He knew she struggled against the increasing weight of responsibility in the organization and yearned for a smaller and simpler portion of life. Though she desired to serve others and give of herself, the life of a Salvation Army officer was arduous. As Shep became more demanding, Debby became more reticent, more withdrawn. It pained him to think of all the nights she would leave their marriage bed, gather her blanket and pillow and go downstairs to sleep.

Perhaps I am like the false portrait of Dorian Gray, he agonized; looking flawless on the exterior, but wrinkled and poisonous on the inside.

Ever the true-blue soldier, Shep reflected that surely he could've done better. Still could, if he got the chance.

Shep also had another failing that he tried to keep to himself, too. But like the hidden poison of Gray it seeped through, tainting his efforts. Though radiantly imaginative, Shep could also be aggressively angry when he was drinking, which he did in secret and to excess. He'd gotten hooked on the saccharine nectar when he was very young, a Catholic altar boy, in fact. A fraction of sweet red wine was always left over in the silver chalices after mass and it became something of a game for Shep to nip some without anyone knowing, then to feel the pleasant buzz of the alcohol in his temples that made everything a little tilted and more fun.

In his frustration at his unaccomplished goals and Debby's seeming reluctance to share his dreams, he was often unkind and hostile to her, pushing her even further away from him.

They tried to keep their problems to themselves and pretend everything was fine: the handsome young leader of the congregation with his lovely songbird wife by his side. But it wasn't fine. It might never be.

Certainly it couldn't have helped their relationship, Shep reflected, that Debby's growing up years were spent with such strange role models for parents: A mother who spent her days propped in a bed in the middle of a room; the walls stacked ceiling-to-floor with thousands of

Harlequin romances, while her husband, now almost completely estranged, resided in the basement. The two never talked directly, but would type messages to each other on an old Remington typewriter permanently perched on the kitchen table.

Debby and Shep's marriage wasn't faring much better. Married almost seventeen years now and with two children, he knew it had been rough sailing for both of them, metaphorically speaking. Though he loved Debby dearly, he couldn't help but wonder if his best choice wouldn't have been to become a Catholic priest after all instead of marrying and seemingly failing at love. Being a priest had almost been his choice.

20

Almost a Priest

Brought up as a good Catholic boy, Shep had memorized the catechism and attended Sacred Heart parochial school with hopes he would continue on through the upper grades at St. Joseph's Academy. At age eight, he learned Latin from Norris Dunfee, an Irish-Catholic bailiff, who every Saturday for a year sat on the church couch and taught Shep syllable by syllable to recite the mass in Latin.

Once proficient, Shep had served mass at the local parish, week in and week out for five years. When a community member died, many were the days Shep was exempted from school for almost a half day to serve at both the requiem mass and at the graveside alongside the local priests. The fragrance of incense and the taste of filched thimbles of communion wine were as familiar to Shep as the smell and flavor of his mother's tamales and salsa.

At the end of Shep's sixth grade year at Sacred Heart Church, he was offered an opportunity to attend a Claretion seminary preparatory school in Calabasas, California. This was a "try-it-on-and-see" priests' school for some of the bright and shining young stars of the

Catholic Church. It seemed to be in good order for this young man, inasmuch as Shep was but a babe-in-arms when his little Mexican grandmother pronounced in no uncertain terms that "this one" would be a priest. Furthermore, Shep was accomplished at reciting the altar boys' portion of the mass, so it seemed a logical step for him to spend a summer exploring the monastic life. One other conscript was chosen to attend with him: one of Shep's classmates, Norbert Wagner.

Thus it was, that Norbert and Shep found themselves walking the palatial corridors of the Malibu Canyon Home for Priests that summer of 1968. They would spend these nine weeks in exploratory classes on catechism, at recruitment lectures, doing exercises that taught them the discipline of becoming a Claret, in athletic activities such as soccer and baseball, and eating sumptuous meals in concentration and silence with fellow seekers at interminably long refectory tables. If it weren't for the abundance of food, Shep would have felt himself akin to Dickens's orphaned Oliver.

One dark night after Lights Out, though Shep knew talk was forbidden, he thought of something he needed to say to Norbert. Speaking in a whisper, his small cot only a four-foot aisle away, Shep began imparting some ideas for the boys' next day's activities. Without the slightest whisper of robes, there suddenly appeared above Shep's cot a secret service branch Claretion. Standing threateningly in the dim light like the dark specter of the Grim Reaper himself, it spoke, saying, "This is a place of learning and only through discipline and devotion can we truly be cleansed."

The Reaper then advised Shep to remove himself from his bunk. As he tumbled obediently to the floor, the specter instructed him to kneel on his own fingers on the cold, hard marble floors.

"I'll be back later," the Reaper said menacingly. "Stay here and pray. Contemplate your actions and formulate what you will do to correct your trespasses."

For the next thirty minutes, which seem no less than several hours, Shep's body seemed to gain a hundred and fifty pounds, all resting on his delicate young fingers, crushing them to numbness. Finally, the robed specter returned. With not a word, he motioned the physically and spiritually chilled boy back to his cot.

What on earth kind of group is this?! Shep queried the silent dark as his swollen fingers slowly regained feeling. They certainly have a strict God around here….

Before sunrise, it had dawned on Shep that he would not become a priest. Nothing personal, he'd concluded, he just couldn't buy into such a harsh program.

The next day, the students were granted a long, "free" day from lunch to 5 p.m. Thus it was that one desperate adolescent decided to leave the seminary in his proverbial dust that very afternoon. Not wanting to face the hierarchy of the seminary, Shep had decided it would be in his best interest to merely walk his way back to Los Angeles and telephone home. At lunch he stocked up, eating hardy for what he knew would be a long journey. Moments after dismissal, Shep slipped into his room, grabbed a jacket, then headed across the soccer field to the back of the spacious seminary property. Seeing a large stand of bamboo growing densely at the fence line, he looked back to see if he'd been observed before clambering through the bamboo and emerging on the other side. To his surprise, beyond the hedge there was nothing: no houses, no cars, and no people, just the rolling hills of the back canyon. What there was, however, was one lone strand of railroad track sitting on a cinder bed, its rails glinting in the mild California sunshine. Looking left, then right, Shep deliberated briefly, checked the sun for position overhead, then took off heading east.

Following the tracks and keeping a fast pace for an hour, Shep refused to think of time or miles, but wondered about God and whether He requires people to do such things as self-inflicted pain. For some reason this above all else seemed incongruous with what he sensed to be true about the Great and Eternal. He cried silently as he walked at a feverish lick, feeling confused over reconciling others' expectations for him toward the priesthood and considering his own ambitions for whatever might lay over the horizon.

Who am I really? Shep pondered. I only want to do the right thing.

The sun beat down on his back as he toiled mercilessly along with no emerging sign of civilization.

About three that afternoon judging from the sun, Shep slowed to a snail's pace then stopped. Straining to see what might be far, far down the tracks, he realized that although he saw nothing definitive, he was surely making great time. About-facing, he again strained to see a sign of the despised seminary. Nothing. But at that very moment, one thing became more clear to Shep than even not wanting to be a priest: if he walked, jogged or ran back down these hot tracks, it was possible he might make it back to the seminary undetected and no one need know of this escapade toward freedom but he and The Man Upstairs, whom he was confident would not require any knuckle-kneeling in connection with this incident.

The rest of his days at the Home for Priests passed quickly and it was soon time to return home. The balance of his seminary experience had gone well and Shep could see the value of proper training for the priesthood, despite the fact he could not see himself as Father Shepard. He thought to himself that before departing he should get with one of the higher-ups, such as the Monsignor or some type of Father Superior, and at least give him his input. It would be along the lines of, "You have a really good school here, but you might consider having girls. It would be a definite improvement. Trust me, Father, on this."

Shep rather believed the original commandment had been *celebrate*, not *celibate*.

21

Love Rounds the Bend

Shep didn't choose the priesthood and he did marry. He met his wife-to-be in the first year of officers' training school -- a somewhat shy, rural girl from Boise, Idaho. They'd felt an instant attraction as they eyed each other discretely across the table at a school dinner. Debby Leatherman was a dedicated would-be missionary who came from a strong Assembly of God background. In her teen years, she had become acquainted with the work of the Salvation Army. She was a befreckled lass with a generously wide mouth and long flowing auburn hair that extended to her waist, which she caught up into a silky bun for official occasions.

Shep and Debby began spending inordinate amounts of time together, walking the San Francisco streets hand-in-hand and riding the romantic trolley cars.

Luckily, Debby was also a happy addition to the Dave/Shep duo, chumming about with them when invited.

She also sang.

A fraternal twin, Debby had been brought up singing church hymns in choirs, duets, or trios, her rich alto voice ringing strong and true. She had even been a member of a trio that had recorded a commercial gospel album featuring regional singers. From the very first church meeting, Shep and Debby found a sweet harmony making music together. By the second semester, they were singing duets during morning devotions and vesper services. As the two years progressed, they found great solidarity in their joint commitment towards the work and purpose of the Salvation Army. They often talked of marriage and being stationed in some third world country together, where they could minister to the needs of their fellow man.

Finding in each other a worthy companion on all levels, Shep and Debby married within a year of graduating, celebrating with a ceremony in a third-story sanctuary in Chinatown overlooking the San Francisco bay.

Bound in a common cause, the couple pastored three separate churches with good success. Shep made several trips to Central America for international relief efforts, laboring alongside other Salvation Army officers in those grief-stricken countries, while Debby remained at home caring for their two children and carrying on their joint duties in his absence.

But time took its toll on the marriage. Though they met with brilliant success in their spiritual work, as individuals, Shep and Debby became more and more distant from each other. Disillusionment and resentment weighed down their relationship. As it stood now, Shep was quite sure that he and Debby would divorce after he returned from the sea.

That was the one thing Dave and Shep had not discussed yet. Shep had been unabashedly envious of Dave and Eva's harmony through the years, their singleness of purpose, but even more, he envied their deep love and devotion to each other. Conversely, he found himself in an empty shell of a marriage. Unbeknownst to Shep, one of the main reasons Dave had wanted to go on this crossing was to help Shep figure out the problems in his marriage. It hurt him that his best friend was so unhappy in his life's partnership. He felt it was Shep's responsibility to make it work.

As the Crossing neared reality, Debby had said nothing. It seemed to Shep as if she truly didn't care whether he went, or whether he would return. Walking out of their apartment that day in May, his sea duffle heavy on his shoulders, the two had shared no animosity, nor had they shared a fond farewell.

In this matter, Shep lived on nervous energy on the ocean, hoping that upon his return somehow he and his wife could begin again and do it better than before.

22

Tumultuous Childhood

Dave's spiritual life had not been as pat from the beginning as Shep's. Raised in a violent household with three older brothers, there was a lot of yelling and even beatings from their British father who drank too much, worked too hard, and loved women other than his wife too much, though he loved her, too.

Dave and his brothers lived in fear of their father. The slightest disorder in the house would cause him to explode, striking out at anyone within reaching distance. Young Dave would flee to the closet, hiding among the musty shoes and dust bunnies, arms crossed against his chest, hoping against hope that nobody would find him there. The walls would reverberate with the intensity of his father's booming, angry voice. For the rest of his life, Dave would dislike raised voices. Many years later and with two sons of his own, Dave returned home for a visit. As he walked to the front door, he could hear his father and stepmother yelling. Loading Ben and Hans back into the car, Dave drove around for an hour before coming back.

"Yelling was part my daily life when I was a kid," he told his boys, "but it will never be part of yours."

His parents divorced when Dave was eight. His most prominent memory was sitting on a judge's lap and having to choose between his parents for Thanksgiving: stay with his mom for the holiday, or ride to Oregon with his dad.

"I had to choose Mom," he recalled. "It would've killed her, if I'd gone with Dad."

Dave loved his big, exuberant, "life of the party" father, nonetheless.

Dave knew that he had a good heart, but was not a good father. He also knew that he, Dave, had a springboard temper just like his father's and he was terrified to pass it on. Believing it was safer not to have children than to lose control, it was six long years after he and Eva married before he could let go of that fear and consent to having children.

But something good came from Dave's pain -- music. Partly as an escape, he began playing music to drown out the violent reverberations of his home life. He learned to play the trombone at age twelve and loved its beautiful, competing sound. By the time he was a long-armed teen, Dave was plying his slender musician's fingers on a Wurlitzer keyboard in a garage band with a friend named Skip, Skip's wife, and a few other guys. They got gigs in nightclubs and at sock hops playing jazz, rock, and Tijuana Brass tunes. Being on stage was like breathing to Dave. When he'd put away his instruments it was almost a physical pain. He imagined death to be very like *not* playing music.

But insecurity was a by-product of his violent home life, too. Handsome and debonair, the girls flocked to Dave. Never without a girlfriend -- afraid to be without one -- he'd become explosively jealous on the turn of a dime. When he would be playing in the band, it was an agony for him to watch "his girl" dancing with another guy.

Over and over Dave had the same nightmare, and it would throw him into panic attacks. He'd be rowing in a small boat. Rowing and rowing until his arms would feel like breaking off, but he knew he couldn't stop because he'd be alone. For years, Dave didn't know why the dream terrified him so much and exactly what it meant.

When asked about his childhood, Dave would make up stories about his memories, talking about events that had happened that really hadn't, and conversely making up events that hadn't happened that he thought had. Even he didn't know for sure what was real. It wasn't until Dave was in his thirties that he found his true memories -- at a prayer meeting in Ecuador.

He'd gone with a group of Jesus Freak friends to share the Word with the uninitiated when, "I just saw it…saw that I'd made so much of my painful childhood up," he recalled. "It hurt like hell to realize I had been living in complete denial."

Particularly painful was a memory of when he was six years old.

"What I remembered was that I was holding on to my dad's leg to keep him from going out and driving drunk," he confided to one of his new friends. "What was really happening was that Dad was threatening to commit suicide."

Dave's pretend memory was that there was black ice outside, and that's why he was so afraid for his father.

More than twenty years later in that little Ecuadorian prayer meeting, Dave faced the realities of his childhood and was able to cry about it. Amazingly, after his tears dried, he found he was no longer afraid to be alone.

23
A Sailor is Born

Every day after school, the band would meet at Skip's house to rehearse. Skip was a rough diamond, a good guy, but given to extravagant bouts of drug use -- nothing heavy usually, just grass and an occasional snort of cocaine. But one day Dave noticed that Skip wasn't doing any drugs.

"What's up?" Dave asked, as casually as he could.

"I'll show you," Skip replied.

By way of explanation, he took Dave to a meeting at High Bridge Park where a Jesus Movement was underway with barefoot flower children singing and praying.

"It's so peaceful and they seem so happy," Dave had whispered to Skip.

Dave knew something was amiss in his life, that was certainly no mystery, and this new way of living an old gospel appealed to him like no other had.

So, on a chilly day in May, 1970, as a worship band gathered at the river bank playing, "Bathed in the Blood of Jesus," Dave was baptized in the cold waters of the Spokane river by a gentle giant of a man purposefully and ironically nicknamed, "Tiny." Rising from the waters of conversion everything in Dave's life began to change; colors seemed brighter, his heart was lighter. For the first time the Bible made sense to him and he began to share its word. Dave dropped out of the raucous rock band. He became obsessed with spreading this new belief of his with the Jesus People; witnessing on street corners, at a skid row coffee house, laying hands on the ill, and volunteering at youth camps to spread the Word. He felt it was one of the greatest gifts of his life.

At the coffee house one day, a gospel compatriot suggested they should disband and go to church. It was a simple matter of deduction for Dave: The Salvation Army was the closest church nearby. It was right there on skid row. Wearing ratty jeans and a scruffy T-shirt, Dave walked in the doors of the church. To his great joy, he found a full brass band belting out gospel hymns on the stage. He'd come home.

I can praise Jesus and *play my trombone,* he grinned to himself, feeling halfway to heaven already; and the Salvation Army praised the Lord that this young Hippy boy had jumped on their wagon -- he was bold with the message and they desperately needed another trombone player.

Years later as a minister, Dave would recall with clarity the exact moment when he knew preaching would be his career.

"Dave, what are you going to do with your life?" a tousled-headed kid asked him one day at a youth camp where Dave was counseling.

Meaning to say that he was going to be a studio musician in L.A., instead Dave replied, "I'm going to be a minister."

Something like that had never occurred

consciously to him before, but as soon as it was out of his mouth he knew it was true.

Surprisingly, it would be his ill-tempered father who would give Dave another of the greatest gifts of his life: an eight-foot green El Toro sailboat with green and yellow striped sails. When Dave's parents divorced, he had gone to live with his father, now shaky but sober. Since motorized boats were not allowed on the lake near his father's new home, the two would climb into the little sailboat, his large father sitting on the center bench for ballast. That unfortunate seat often put him in direct line of the boom, which smacked him to the side of the head more than once as the two began learning the rudiments of corralling the shifting wind in the canvas sails.

So it was that the glistening of the water sliding so enigmatically beneath the boat, and the slip of her through the breeze, exhilarated young Dave. He wanted nothing more than to become a sailor.

After school the next week, he stopped by the town's only library and found a book on how to set the rigging; how to go against a perpendicular wind, and more.

Like a sponge, Dave soaked up the diagrams and instructions, saying to himself, *Oh, so* that's *how you do it…* only to find out later in actually sailing that it never really worked out the way he'd read it would.

When the lake would freeze over from November to March, Dave lamented the loss of a chance to sail, substituting ice fishing on the lake instead. He never wished to be far from the water or the warehouse where

El Toro was snugged up for the winter.

As if trying to make up for all the years he had been a bad father, Dave's dad also introduced him to midget racecar driving and snow skiing. But it was sailing that captured the boy's imagination and heart.

For the rest of his life, Dave would never be without a sailboat, except while he was in training college, and though he didn't own one then, he was always able to find the time and means to rent a boat and sail at one of the nearby lakes. To say sailing was in his blood would be a gross understatement of fact. Dave was, by his own admission, "made for the ocean." When he first caught sight of it at the Ocean Shores Beach outside Puget Sound in Washington when he was fifteen, Dave fell to his knees and sobbed at its beauty.

For the rest of his life, Dave intended never to live more than a few miles from the ocean. It was his sanctuary where no one could hurt him and he was free from the pressure he always felt to help other people. Whether in Seattle, Santa Monica, Long Beach, or San Diego, Dave always chose his procession of homes because of their proximity to his beloved ocean.

24
Medicinal Minerals

After two weeks on the ocean the seas simply died beneath the boat. The ebb and flow of water ceased and it seemed as if the earth had stopped spinning. The silence became overwhelming. For days on end, no wind whatsoever fluffed the sails above Mini. They hung limp from the mast, not stirring from their ropes. The men dripped with sweat from the humidity and felt like prisoners locked in cumbersome chains: two men, a hundred square feet of living space, and going absolutely nowhere.

The two wracked their brains for something to do. The novelty of plunking on small instruments had worn off. Shep was out of skits for the moment. They were sick of cards. Shep decided to take a bath, if only for diversion not necessarily for cleanliness.

Regular bathing on Mini was a strange ritual in itself accomplished by getting completely naked and sitting on the bench of the small cockpit, where the non-bathing man would unceremoniously pour a five-gallon bucket of salt brine and seawater over the bather's head. Then, if so inclined, the bather could take a bar of soap and smear himself with paste. But since seawater doesn't lather, it would merely cover the bather with a milky film. At this point, abrading one's skin with a brush was sometimes a comfort, particularly if any sores had shown up from the constant salt water eddying around ankles confined in saltwater-trapping boots, or arm pits where the constant rubbing of clothing also trapped the scratchy water and caused salt burns. Ironically, scrubbing with a little salt could relieve the discomfort, thus proving that two negatives *can* make a positive.

On this particularly dull, but sunny mid-ocean morning as Shep began to ready for his bath, he reached into his duffle bag and his hand bumped against a quart-sized jar of foreign mud sealed with a rubber gasket and sporting a fancy logo. It was some type of medicinal trace mineral-enriched mud from the Dead Sea in Israel. He remembered buying it at some wayside vendor near an area where people came from all over the world to pack themselves with this mud. Although not usually given over to gimmicks, Shep had purchased this jar of mud as a souvenir; something practical to take home from his trip, yet over the ensuing ten years he'd never used it. For some odd reason, the night he was throwing his bag together in San Francisco readying to head south, it had caught his eye and for no good reason, he'd tossed it into the bag.

Suddenly, Shep had an idea. Carrying the jar out of the cabin and grinning like the Cheshire cat, he screwed off the sealed lid. The escaping air hissed like a jungle snake. Shep dipped his hand into the silky black silt of mud from another ocean away. He smoothed the chocolate mud over his forehead, cheeks, around his nose and across his chin. It felt like a suede coat of armor against the sun, as over his ears and down his tanned neck went another swath of mud. With both hands, he kneaded the sludge between his fingers and spread it across his smooth chest.

"Eureka," he called back down to Dave. "I've found a glorious ointment for anything that ails you today, my friend: sunburn, chapping, blisters, abdominal cramps…."

Looking through the gangway and seeing a black mud monster above, both curious and dubious, Dave asked, "What in the world are you doing?"

"I'm taking the cure," Shep chortled, continuing to smear mud all the way to his knees. Meanwhile, the concoction on his forehead was drying, turning from black to a light gray color and beginning to crack.

It's hard to comprehend how much mud those ingenious Israelites were able to pack into one wide-mouth quart jar, he marveled.

There must be gallons in here, Shep thought, as he raised his arms and rubbed the mud into his hair, then bent down and finished off the treatment by slapping the mud around his ankles and between his toes.

By this time, Dave had emerged from below and was well ready for this strange hygienic routine. Dousing himself with seawater, adding a little scrubbing and another rinse, he said to Shep, "Gimme that jar."

Sliding it gingerly across the cockpit with his foot, Shep was careful not to let any sudden movement crack his perfectly mummified body.

"Wait till you start baking," Shep sighed. "You're gonna love it."

It was hard to say whether mud heated you up or cooled you down, Dave thought, *but this fact was for sure, it protected a person from the burning of the sun as surely as a clay sarcophagus.*

Sunburns were a way of life on ship. No part of the exposed body was safe from the sun's red hot rays. Even though Shep and Dave always wore hats, the reflection of sun off the flat surface of the water had even cooked the tender skin under their chins raw. But here they were, lounging fully exposed in their birthday suits in the glare of the noonday sun, yet perfectly comfortable. Looking like naked Aboriginals, the men laughed and pointed at each other as they slowly transformed from white boys to earthen gargoyles.

"There goes that mayonnaise skin," Shep snickered to Dave.

"Yeah, well you look 'Black like Me,' Shepper!" Dave retorted.

But for sure, the healing had begun, just like it said on the jar: "Medicinal Mineral Treatment."

At last the two had found a way to celebrate this void in their trip, having nothing better to do. It was a great joy to simply lay prone in their earthen cloaks like lazy lizards on a sun-drenched rock, all the while feeling they should be beating on drums or blowing on didgeridoos in keeping with their new skin tone. Instead they lay back on each bench side of the cockpit in complete relaxation. Basting in the sun for an hour till they felt done, it was the first time in days they'd truly enjoyed themselves.

Finally, Dave sat up straight, leaned over the side of the boat, and slid headfirst into the bathtub-warm water. Swirling slowly around, a cloud of dark gray murky water rose from his body like a miniature galaxy spreading outwards before dispersing into the motionless sea. Sinking down, then rising up for a gasp of air, down he went again, up again, rinsing, then rinsing again. Finally getting his original color back and feeling as squeaky clean as if from a fresh bath, Dave hoisted himself up by the side rail and slipped back into boat.

Meanwhile, Shep, the old land crab, was hesitant to get out of the boat like his buddy Dave, whom he secretly believed was surely part merman, so he rinsed his mud off with the bucket, sending gallon after gallon of murky water out through the scuppers and into the ocean.

As the two dried off in the warm sun, they concluded that mud is wonderful stuff -- only problem: there's never enough.

Within a few days, the men once again found themselves bored to the point of tension, so Dave decided it was time to go underwater and give the boat a thorough examination.

A small underwater device attached to Mini's hull with a small plastic impellor measured the distance the boat had traveled. It had somehow jammed and was no longer giving their distance with any accuracy.

"C'mon, Shep. Don the gear. We're goin' down," Dave said.

Normally, the men would do this job in tandem: one in the ocean, one in the boat, just to be on the safe side. But this time, Captain Dave determined the two should descend together.

With every shred of sail rolled tight, the helm lashed hard to port so nothing could take this boat away and leave them mortally stranded, they prepared to take the dive. Stripping to the skin, Dave reached into a cubby and produced a custom-made diving mask upon which the prescriptions from his eyeglasses had been ground into a superb thick face glass through which he could read his wristwatch under water or see to make any number of necessary and delicate repairs.

Shep strapped on a regular clear facemask. Sliding the leather belt from his trousers, he put it over his head and under one arm diagonally, then tucked a diving knife beneath it close to his chest. Protected thus, he could patrol the perimeter and allow Dave to make the repairs without constantly looking over his shoulder for potential danger.

With arched backs, the men tumbled over the sides and into the water. The rays of the sun penetrated downward, creating a lovely aqua glow around Mini's hull. At port, she had been painted with two coats of anti-fouling marine paint that showed up shiny black beneath the water line, making her twin keels resemble the fins of a killer whale lazily floating at rest on top of the ocean.

Dave dove deep then rose slowly, looking up at the hull. Shep circled the boat, surveying its profile. Dave began to swim upside down, bumping along the bottom of the hull and running his hands over the black surface, knocking loose any debris or build-up from kelp, plankton, or any number of microscopic sea creatures that abounded in these waters.

In the mid-portion of the Pacific there is no sign of life anywhere. With little conjuring, one's skin could crawl from the indelible impression left by Steven Spielberg's terror evoking, "Jaws."

This is spooky, Shep thought, a quiver traveling down his spine.

Like a naked jellyfish, slowly, almost motionlessly, he continued circling, watching. It wasn't long until he became anxious for air. As he looked up before surfacing, there above him was a solid blanket of angel hair-looking plankton coating the ocean surface. Hanging in long strands a fraction the thickness of a human hair, the sunlight shown down through the tubes in a surreal display of brightness visible only by looking up from ten to fifteen feet below the ocean surface.

Now, that's *a magic trick,* Shep thought.

Swimming through the plankton to the surface, he coughed slightly before refilling his lungs and pushing downward once again. Dave continued his methodical work, holding the oxygen in his lungs without needing a re-supply of air.

Good grief, Dave must be a sea creature with gills instead of lungs, Shep mused.

It was strange that with the sunlight penetrating so deeply into the water, Shep felt free in an environment he'd always feared. He reached across his chest and toyed with the handle of his elegant skin diver's knife. Unable to resist the temptation, he unsheathed it and flashed it back and forth through the watery sun, noting how the silver shaft shone back up against the surface. For a minute, Shep forgot his true gentle nature and wished against all odds that a feeding hammerhead shark might pass this way soon.

All the while, the skipper continued to run his hands over Mini's keels, checking and re-checking the condition of all the modifications he'd made months before. Then, bumping gracefully out from under Mini, more like an aquarium seal than a man, Dave moved to the top.

"How do you do that?" Shep asked, knitting his brows in wonder.

"What?"

"Hold your breath for fifteen minutes!"

"Holding your breath for a long time is all about being at ease in the ocean, whether above it or below it," Dave replied.

Funny, Shep thought. *That was rather how Dave lived his religion, too. Once found, it was as if he'd never been without it; swimming in the element of his love for it as if he'd been born there.*

25
More than Tuna

From the beginning, there was never a question but that the two men would be friends; fast friends for life. They had endless admiration for each other, to the point of sometimes wishing they were not themselves, but the other. But even in the most ideal of relationships, differences can at times rear an ugly head. Being at sea was an extreme testing. Like two tigers caged together for too long, things could erupt and did on occasion. One of those times was on a sunny Sunday as Shep was on deck whipping up his Super-Duper-Extraordinary tuna sandwiches. Dave emerged from the cabin just as Shep was chopping some pickles into the final mix.

"No, no, no. Yuk!" Dave exclaimed. "Pickles don't go in tuna fish!"

"Of course pickles go in tuna fish," Shep retorted. "Are you nuts? What's tuna without pickles?"

The exchange went back and forth, becoming more heated by the minute. Finally, taking all he could endure of Shep's superior attitude, Dave spat out, "You do not have the definitive answer on everything. ("Definitive" was Dave's favorite word.) "You don't know everything!"

It was about more than the tuna.

Shep had his maternal grandfather Moreno's blazing temperament as well as a who-knew-where-it-came-from charisma, and he could fly from one to the other with a swiftness Dr. Jekyll and Mr. Hyde would envy. A human chameleon, his charm could light up a room or his anger extinguish the very air. He walked a fine line between his dazzling magnetism and his rage. And to top it off, with a kind of unaware arrogance, Shep believed he *did* have all the answers. If someone disagreed with him on anything from the weather to religious doctrine, he was known to come back with an undiplomatic, "You're wrong."

Though the power of Shep's personality could be his greatest attraction, on Mini's deck, Dave was not entranced. He was enraged. All the small irritations that had been broiling inside him in regards to his friend charged out with bayonets raised. This particular fight had begun brewing long before lunch, and in fact even before last night, when Shep had innocently offered, "If you need any help unhooking the bowlines, tell me."

Dave thought Shep was being demeaning.

"The day I need sailor-help from you, I'll have a peg leg and a hook!" Dave had answered. "You are such an elitist! Not only does everything come so easily to you from friends to school, you always think you're right."

"What?!" Shep had shot back. You...you...*you* have everything so easy! You have the perfect life: a loving wife, a home of your own...heck, you even have your own church!"

"It's not that hard, Shep," Dave retorted. "You just have to work at it." By that, he meant work at the marriage.

The meaning was not lost on Shep.

"I *have* worked on it! I *do* work on it! It's just no use. We're too different."

"Maybe if you'd stop drinking and trying to control everything and allow Debby to have her own opinions and goals, that might help," Dave said, his anger cooling.

Mollified beyond hurt, Shep knew Dave was right, and he once again committed to making his marriage work when he hit shore.

26

Target Practice

The doldrums continued. At the risk of killing each other, the friends continued searching for things with which to entertain themselves.

For years, Shep had owned a Charter Arms Survival rifle, a basic 22-guage rifle; the kind that breaks down, tucks into its own hollow stock and at that point is impervious to water damage. It was not a sophisticated or expensive rifle, simply a minimalist novelty. Shep had brought it along in case of a disaster; such as a shark, or other unexpected survivalist experience.

Ammunition was cheap: fifty rounds to a box, so he'd brought a brick, which totaled twenty-five boxes. Without any danger to speak of insight, but dying from the monotony, the two occasionally brought out the gun and assembled it. In the shank of an afternoon when time was slow and entertainment sparse, they'd sit in the cockpit and shoot aimlessly at the horizon.

"Betcha I can beat you in a contest," Shep challenged, finding the horizon a tasteless target.

"Yeah, bring it on, big boy," Dave retorted.

They spent fifteen minutes scavenging things to shoot at that would float: an egg that had gone bad in the heat, an orange peel, part of a potato. They tossed them off the stern one at a time. As the chosen object floated away, each took a turn plinking at it. Sometimes one of them even got lucky.

"Ha-ha. Gotcha!" Dave chortled, as he blasted an apple core apart.

"Oh, c'mon," Shep countered. "You really think that beat that old juice carton I exploded?!"

But more often than not the contest consisted merely of competing to see who could come closest, judging by splashes in the vicinity of the object. They'd slowly shoot one box of ammo at a time, saving the rest for another day.

"Sure glad we had *this* on this list," Dave said, with a big smile.

It was actually rare to see the two men compete at anything. Shep conceded that Dave was always better at virtually everything except, perhaps, scholarship. Though Dave had studied feverishly for exams and done well, Shep never studied. He spent his evenings riding streetcars and observing people, yet had still earned good grades.

"I hated you for that," David confessed one lazy summer day, recalling time after time that he'd left the bulletin board posted with theological test results bearing a grim expression and clenched fists. Once again, Shep had bested him on paper.

"Of course, I really was just jealous," he added, grinning over at Shep. "What did you have…osmosis, or something? You just seemed to absorb information without studying."

"Yeah, yeah, like there's one other thing I do better than you," Shep said, believing he'd never known a man as multi-talented as Dave. "You beat me at everything else."

It was clear they envied each other's oppositeness, translated it to esteem, and silently wished they could be more like the other.

27

Albatross of Luck

A t three o'clock one sultry afternoon a lone albatross visited the men. At any time that would have been a rare event, even more so considering they were now eight hundred miles from California with no land before Hawaii.

"Where is that big guy going?" Dave speculated. "Where, other than on us or the water, can he land?"

It was obvious that on this bird's long-winged trek, it was as surprised to see the men as they were to see it. With a wingspan nearing twelve feet, the white giant hovered on the air currents above Mini's masts, silently watching the sailors.

Shep dashed below, turning round and round in the tiny cabin trying to find a piece of bread or something to offer the seemingly errant bird.

"What do you feed a sea bird anyway?" he hollered up the gangway. "He's got to be hungry and in need of companionship. We certainly are."

Meanwhile, Dave was making bird sounds and calmly trying to coax the bird nearby, somehow naively believing that this great creature of land and sea would come down and land right on their cabin like a long-lost acquaintance.

After a long, leery pause observing the men and their inscrutable antics, the nomadic bird flew a safe distance from their vessel and put down on his own flotation.

Somehow the men felt even lonelier than before. As they turned away from the aloof bird their longing for home pinched like a shoe worn one size too small.

Lowering the brim on his hat to better shade his face, Dave gazed down at his wedding band, its gold and silver circle etched with the letters, "D & E," and PIUS, the Hebrew word for Christ. He thought for the umpteenth time how much he missed Eva and the boys, even more than he'd thought he would. Strange...at home he hardly noticed if they were there sometimes as he plodded around his study reading his books; perusing that one then another, then fiddling on the computer or jotting notes for next week's sermon. From the rattle of dishes or the distant sound of one of the boy's stereos playing, he knew Eva and the kids were there. He'd have never guessed what a comfort those vague noises would have been right now.

Shep lounged lengthwise on the starboard cockpit bench and likewise was lost in thoughts of home. Gosh. It was Friday, wasn't it? Yeah. If he were home right now, he and Mandy and little John would be bicycling out for pizza on what they called, "TGI Friday." After the last crust had been abandoned on their plates, they'd head home and watch, "All in the Family," their favorite sitcom on TV.

Just then it hit him -- it was Debby's birthday.

"Hey, Dave. Time for a celebration...it's my wife's birthday today!"

"Of course! Okay, hang on."

Down Dave went to the cabin and up he came with his tin whistle.

Soon, "Happy birthday to you, happy birthday to you…" was echoing off the drooping sails as the men celebrated in a small way the events they were missing at home. They were missing a lot of those events. Debby, Mandy and John were all having birthdays while Shep was away on the Crossing, and so was Ben. For each and every one, the men would sing "Happy Birthday," and sometimes they'd even stick an emergency candle into a warm MRE to really kick up the celebration.

28
Who's Biting?

One of the pieces of equipment Dave had decided to take on the trip was a hydro-odometer, a brass clock of sorts that would hook to the back rail of the transom and trail behind the ship on a 50-foot length of heavy, cotton lanyard. A spiral arrow would spin the lanyard in the water as the boat moved forward. In turn, the lanyard would wind the gear in the clock, advancing the mileage. Considered to be fairly accurate, the device was an antique compared to modern plastic digital devices that performed a similar function. Thus, it was somewhat precious to the person who loaned it to Dave Chamberlain, but they knew Dave would certainly return it to them in good shape and so parted with it kindly.

Earlier on the voyage, Dave had installed the piece and it had been ticking along for some days keeping faithful track of Mini's mileage.

Shep had taken up fishing sometime earlier, as well, and at all times was floating bright lures that bobbed and glinted in the sun 100- to 150-feet from the boat. He changed them with regularity to see if he could lure in a fish. Surprisingly, at no time in the hundreds of miles so far had he gotten so much as the suspicion of a fish having ever passed by. But this particular afternoon, while Shep was wiling away the hours away dangling his pole quietly in the water as Mini sailed along at four or five knots there was an thud, then a vibration, then nothing. At first he thought something had hit the boat, which was highly unlikely, but later when Dave went to check the odometer, he found that the outrigging line of the odometer -- which was made of steel as thick as a man's index finger -- had been sheared off sharply at the end of the lanyard and the precious borrowed odometer was gone.

"This is like a Twilight Zone episode," Dave lamented. "Some large fish with razor-sharp teeth had to have bitten it off."

"Geez. So, what are my bright fishing lures…chopped liver?" Shep said, peeved. "I can't believe they preferred your flashy odometer instead."

It was the only known fish bite during the entire trip and the borrowed odometer had gone for fish food.

Then there was the day Shep saw The Box.

Along about mid-day, as he was lazily strumming his guitar outside on the portside bench, he happened to look down. In mid-ocean the water is clear as glass, unlike the murky depths near land, and there he saw a huge cargo box still in its net passing beneath the boat. It had undoubtedly broken free from a transport ship and was floating only five to six feet below the boat.

That's eerie, Shep thought. It's so gigantic and out of place. How shocking as well, he realized with a shudder, that the highly buoyant, 30-plus-foot square box could've easily sunk Mini's small 20-foot length in a whisper and the men would've never known what hit them.

Luckily, the box drifted just far enough below to miss their precious keels.

The ocean can be a huge and vastly silent place to be, where one thinks surely they are absolutely alone in the world. Late one night, Shep looked up from his watch at the helm as the clouds floated gently aside and the skies opened for just a few moments. He saw high in the sky the dot of a commercial airliner heading due west. It caught him by surprise as he was sure at this longitude and latitude that Mini couldn't possibly be in a regular commercial flight corridor.

With the small boat so isolated and with such an absence of any distraction or noise, Shep cocked his head and listened for the rumble of the engines high above. Disappointed, he heard nothing. Apparently, the huge jet was flying at such a high altitude that on his lonely night watch Shep could only remember what it would sound like.

While Dave slept peacefully in the cabin, Shep remained alone at the tiller, but in his mind's eye he pictured himself sitting on his quarter berth, looking across to the opposite wall of Mini's cabin. There he saw the small emergency signaling device. Shep couldn't help but wonder that if that signal were sending would anybody actually hear it? For a moment, he daydreamed about the sound of a mayday crackling through, or a pulsating SOS. As his eyebrows almost met each other in a scrunch, he wondered if they sent one out how would anybody actually hear it in this great, empty place?

His awareness returned to the tiller and the smells of the night air. He looked up again to the mast light, which had now disappeared from sight masked by the billowing sail, and he hoped they'd never have to test it.

Soon we will be in the halfway spot exactly, if that spot can be measured at all. Many people do not realize that the Pacific Ocean is the largest water body in the world and that because of the placement of the Hawaiian islands at mid-Pacific, it is a location farthest from land on the earth, Shep wrote in his diary. *It's a place so isolated you would have to actually leave the planet to be any more alone.*

Mini was not radio-equipped by nautical standards, having only a common CB radio with a daytime distance -- accounting for solar interference -- of only fourteen miles, give or take a few. However, at night, when there was no intrusion from the solar static, the radio could have a maximum range of as many as sixty miles. As they reached the midpoint of the ocean, about 1,200 miles off the California coast, Shep pictured a round net sixty miles wide, reaching out from them in every direction and thought what a vast amount of ocean they were touching at that moment. Going down below where Dave was reading, Shep reached to the radio and pressed the button. He called out, then waited to hear a response from another vessel.

"Any vessel. Calling any vessel. This is California sailing ship Mini C5623. Hailing any vessel. Please answer. *Please.*"

In the darkness of her cabin the two men sat, listening, waiting. No sound returned. Like fishermen throwing out a net and pulling it back empty, time and again Shep threw out the call, waited, threw it out again, waited once again.

Across the very middle of their journey -- the middle one hundred miles -- late into the evening and into the night they took turns calling out into the darkness. Each time their call went unanswered.

Finally, clicking off the radio, Dave said, "Do you realize, Shep, that as far as we know, we are the only two human hearts beating out here?"

29

Shriekers and Temptations

T he small Christian college where Dave and Shep met was at the corner of Geary and Laguna Street in the Fillmore District of San Francisco, probably the most colorful place any theology students could be during the years of 1973 and 1974. In those two years alone, the People's Temple and Jim Jones relocated from there to Guyana; Patricia Hearst was abducted by the Simbionese Liberation Army; and one of the most militant Black Muslim movements and its temple was approximately three blocks down the street. A myriad of other religious groups proliferated around the troubled area of the Fillmore, and it was not uncommon for the Salvation Army students to go outside their gate to catch the Muni bus and find themselves standing between three nuns and several Hari Krishna worshippers as they waited to board. Perhaps a couple of Buddhist monks would be stepping off the bus as they got on.

Because Dave and Shep were theology students they were interested in other denominations and sects around the training college, which was a wild mix of ethnic groups and cultures with Orientals, Blacks, Whites, and a mix of a mix thereof. The boys often went out on their own to investigate places such as the Islamic temple, or the Four-square Church in the Black section -- checking out some of the most extreme religions in the area just to see the differences.

What makes them them and us us? the two wondered. *Is it anything tangible?*

One of the more radical and peculiar movements was the Jesus Shriekers, about which the boys had read on the San Francisco Examiner's religious page. This group followed an Oriental fundamentalist named Witness Lee who had been a student of Watchman Neehis. Late one evening on free time, Dave and Shep slunk incognito down a back alley to a location they'd heard about. In an average-looking Victorian house, they wound down to the basement where the room was packed with the strange Shriekers, who would stand for hours at a time shoulder to shoulder against the walls in the basement listening to nothing more than a Radio Shack cassette player on the floor with an man speaking to them about certain Christian doctrines. In moments of joy and elation, all would yell as loudly as they could. Wide-eyed and close-mouthed, the two young men found the event both humorous and terrifying, though they were reverently fascinated as well.

Another group the boys were interested in checking out was the Nation of Islam farther down Geary about five blocks toward Golden Gate Park. One Saturday evening, hair slicked down and in suits and ties, they climbed the dozen stairs toward the intimidating doorway. Half-dozen surly Black men suddenly blocked their ascent.

"You don't want to be going in here," said one, his arms crossed firmly across his chest.

"But we're just interested in learning about the Nation of Islam," Shep spoke up.

Without saying another word, but with a severe expression, the man gave them to understand that was not possible. And that was that. The boys turned heel and came back the way they'd come. But it would be an eerie echo in their minds some time later when that faction would intersect their lives with tragic results.

The Fillmore District was also a very fleshy area, second only to North Beach and the Tenderloin for its vulgar ways and the boys were often confronted with the peril of life on the streets. On one occasion, Dave had a brush with a very earthy temptation, which he eventually confided to Shep.

The two young men were repairing musical instruments in the shop, when Dave began poring out his experience; the brief struggle he had encountered, and his fear of having breached his own ethics and irreversibly marked his soul.

It seemed that one night Dave was walking down Post Street alone when a beautiful, but scantily clad woman who was obviously "working" the area, approached him.

"Hey, handsome," she beckoned to Dave. "Come on over here and I'll give you a night to remember."

Shocked, Dave hesitated. Then he slowly crossed the street to talk to her.

"Oh, you're a cute one," she crooned; stroking his shoulder and running a hot pink nail down his chest.

Goose bumps sprung up under her hand, as Dave struggled with himself to walk away, when what he really wanted to do was just see what her glossy lipstick would taste like. His mind thrashed about trying to reconcile the situation.

Just then, her hand slid inside his shirt, stopping short at something she felt there. Pulling out the silver cross on a chain that his mother had given him after his baptism, she laughed.

"So, what's this, Jesus boy? A little testing of the faith?" she taunted.

Jerking the cross out of her hands, Dave spun around and ran down the street, not stopping to figure out where he was headed until blocks later. But the fact that he'd hesitated; that he'd considered what it would be like to lay with that woman shamed him.

Shep realized then how incredibly straightforward and utterly above reproach Dave truly was and would always remain. What the circumspect Dave saw as spiritual peril, Shep saw as being no more than the annoyances that come with the reality of man's existence.

Because of their escapades, "which were great and many," they'd joke, the two young men defined more solidly what they believed and why, and grew in their individual faith in God and in each other as encouragers toward their mutual future as clergymen. Both young men would be commissioned as officers and receive their ordination as ministers on the same day. It was a joint ordination of the two in some way, as they felt they had a common yoking together of a shared vision. When Dave and Shep walked from the San Francisco Civic Auditorium that bright spring graduation day, the two felt more a joining than a parting of the way, though in ten hours they would each be on their way to separate parts of the country.

"I love you, brother," Dave said, his voice catching in his throat.

"We'll always be brothers," Shep echoed, feeling the same difficulty with his words.

The following year when Dave wed Eva in Oakland, California, Shep would be his Best Man. That very same year when Shep and Debby wed, Dave was his Best Man.

30

Divergent Paths

Thirty days at sea is an interminably long time to be away from the ones you love and to not have solid earth resounding beneath your feet. It's also a trial to be restricted to a mere hundred square feet of living space on a rocking boat accompanied by another human. No matter the strength of the friendship, it can try one's soul.

It had been almost twenty years to the day since Dave and Shep had gathered their belongings and set off into the wide world from seminary graduation to the day they embarked on the Crossing. During that time, occasions to see each other had been rare: a class reunion; vacationing in the same town as the other's residence; possibly a conference nearby. Otherwise, it had simply been a matter of exchanging annual Christmas letters catching up on the year's activities, a few phone calls from time to time when they felt they could afford it, and the rare letter.

But throughout all that time, they had both kept involved in the work of the ministry and remained open in their communications to each other as life friends do, discussing their children, wives, successes and failures. Once in a while when they happened to be together, they would stay up till the small hours of the morning entertaining each other with stories of their lives, bouncing ideas back and forth, and running important issues through the other's mental sieve, as it were, to process their lives' occurrences and bring the other up to the present. So, for the past two decades, not much had passed under the bridge of each life that the other didn't know about, including some of their most difficult passages.

Within two years of the men's ordinations to the ministry and their first appointments as pastors, Dave had shocked his friend, rocked him really, with the revelation that he was leaving the Salvation Army.

"I can't stay under the yoke any longer, Shep," Dave had said. "It's not really the doctrine, it's the machine itself. It's grinding me down. I'm going out on my own."

Shep was unable to believe Dave could possibly desert the cause to which they had committed together.

"That's not possible, Dave," he'd said in desperation. "You're the rock...the man with the solid foundation.

"This is surely just a phase, Dave. I can't see you as a Gospel gypsy," Shep had continued. "Hang in there, my friend. You'll get over it."

In answer, Dave had silently handed Shep his finest Salvation Army tunic and his ministry ring.

"Keep them, Shep," he said. "I won't be wearing them again."

With heartfelt emotion, Dave revealed, "I don't have any great doctrinal or denominational contentions, but I truly feel in my heart that my original calling is taking me in a new direction."

"You're a far braver man, than I," Shep replied, fighting back tears.

Dave had stuck to his commitment to leave and stepped out in faith to begin an independent church.

In the bay area, Shep enjoyed massive organizational support complete with international offices, promotions and high financing, but watched almost with envy as this lone man with his wife, kids, and naught more than a car, established a church of his heart in the San Diego south bay. He couldn't help admiring Dave's great courage and show of character as he patiently gathered one parishioner at a time, setting stone upon stone in a great soul movement.

Dave would be equally as stunned years down the road when Shep confided in him that he and Debby were likely getting a divorce, something so unthinkable to Shep that it was wrenching for him to speak of it to anyone, let alone admit it to himself. Holding to the highest of family values as well, Dave could in no way embrace such devastating news and it would be the test of the men's friendship, a contest between the iron clad paradigms they both held to and the deep friendship that had grown between them through the years.

But in the end, after years of learning complicated theological doctrine, then practicing it as ministers, Dave and Shep had both come to the conclusion that it ultimately all added up to faith, hope and charity, the simple tenants of a good life. This, they would always have in common, and so to fill some of the long ocean-faring days, Dave and Shep decided they'd each make some symbol of their journey on this endless body of water, this deep bowl of sea, that would represent the time they'd spent here learning about themselves, their faith, and their friendship. It would be a contest with a first place winner and a second. They would make talismans of their voyage.

In ancient mariner tradition, a cross, an anchor, and a heart represented the tenants of faith, hope, and charity. So they would each carve from a square of soft spruce not much bigger than a 50-cent piece, their interpretation of those symbols of the essence of life.

Taking out their small Buck knives, and with all the time in the world and keen eyes, the two bent their heads dutifully over the six small chunks of wood and began. The heart was easy, the cross more difficult because of the wood grain, and the anchor -- virtually impossible. Their fingers seemed thick as baseball bats and as clumsy. The knife would slip off the wood time and again, coming dangerously close to slicing a thigh or a palm. It helped that the two had made the rule that if a piece broke during carving, it was acceptable to glue it back together. Dave became frustrated early on, which was almost funny given that Shep was by nature the restless, impatient one. After snapping his anchor piece time after time, Dave threw up his hands in agony.

"That's it. I'm going to make my anchor out of plywood," he groaned and headed to the cabin to find the coping saw.

Using paper-thin sheets of wood and laminating them together in the approximate size of a half-dollar, Dave was finally able to carve a crude, but substantial anchor.

Once carved, they had to carefully drill holes in the soft wood pieces without cracking all their hard work, then loop the amulets on lanyards to wear around their necks. Always the consummate utilitarian, Dave used a plain white cotton cord for his lanyard, and flamboyant Shep -- in lieu of the gold braid he wished he had -- wove his from nylon rope strands in yellow and blue.

Setting the six small medallions of wood up for display, the men stepped back.

"I'm telling you, that is the finest example of creative woodworking I've ever seen," Shep boasted of his trio.

"Are you kidding me?" Dave replied in mock shock. "*These* three are made by a *true* craftsman. The choice is clearly for my set."

After a squall of words and an acrimonious, but pretend fistfight, the two decided there was no clear winner. With only two judges' opinions it would have to be a tie, though in each man's heart, he thought his was best.

31
Blowin' in the Wind

After seven days of dreary doldrums, early one morning Dave jumped up from his breakfast plate and gazed intently at the sea beyond the boat.

"It's rippling," he mumbled, watching.

"What's rippling, Dave?" Shep asked.

"Hallelujah," Dave cried. "We can sail again! Get that sail ratcheted up, mate!"

"I don't see anything, Dave," Shep said, straining to see what it was Dave was seeing.

"It's wind, Shep. You can see it moving up on us. Trust me. The wind is going to blow!"

Just then, a gust of wind washed over Shep, ruffling his hair, and he remembered what the wind had always meant to him: not sails, but kites.

This ocean breeze reminded Shep of his first spring at the training school when he'd decided to hark back to his childhood days and build a kite of grand proportions. He was thinking about a kite he'd had when he was nine, when one evening his father had brought home a roll-end of heavy brown butcher paper from his job at the Veterans Administration Medical Center. John Jacob had ceremoniously laid the heavy paper on the floor.

"We're going to make a kite, son," he said as he began tracing the silhouette of a coffin. "It'll be a three-stick kite."

To his young son this was a foreign design. Shep had only seen two-stick kites at Woolworth's...the 25-cent ones emblazoned with a Jolly Roger or a unicorn. This plain brown wrapper kite seemed to lack personality altogether, he thought, as he and his father folded and tacked the paper to the sticks with white glue.

Truth be told, Shep was secretly a bit embarrassed and more than a little skeptical of the kite's ability the next day at the Prescott Kiwanis Kite Contest when he and his dad pulled the gigantic paper wing from the back of the family's wood-sided station wagon. The kite was so large it would barely lay flat in the car. When standing next to it Shep was dwarfed. Head to toe, it was the young boy's equal.

Dutifully, Shep dragged the kite across the dry Willow Lake flats to the flying area, its long, torn-sheet tail gathering a furring of large brown cockleburs. Although he was quite sure disaster was only seconds away, Shep hated to let his father down by not participating, so he stood patiently beside the drab brown kite, believing in his heart that they would both go home shamed by the kite's debacle. He could only imagine what the kids would say back at school the next day...kids being kids and all.

That particular Saturday afternoon in March was excessively windy, even for a kite contest. Fathers and sons and daughters held tightly to a wide assortment of predominantly store-bought kites and waited for some Kiwanian to officially signal the start of the contest.

As the whistle trilled its signal to release the kites, Shep was distracted by the number of them snapping about in the hands of would-be launchers, doing double loops, then crashing into the ground and breaking their thin wooden spars on impact. The beautiful paper faces shred into strips as the wind dragged them across the ragged ground, leaving the tattered remains pinioned in nearby bushes.

Shep looked on, stunned by the carnage.

"Shep," his father called, breaking the spell. "Let's get this kite in the air, son."

With a firm, but gentle motion, Shep released the huge paper wing. It lifted smoothly, slowly at first, then gathered speed and suddenly took flight. Its line spun by the yard from the bulky reel of twine, heating Shep's hands to burning as he switched the reel from hand to hand, sending the strong cotton thread to the sky. Climbing quickly to an altitude of 500 to 600 feet in the air, the giant kite leveled off, poised itself above the rest, and danced joyously on the currents for all to see.

Told you so, son, his pragmatic father's matter-of-fact stance seemed to say. Shep stood enchanted, shocked by the kite's unlikely flight. His surprise soon melted into a respectable pride as he held tight to the string and began to pretend he knew all along that a kite of this magnitude could make such a showing. For the next half hour, young Shep was the recipient of many compliments and good wishes as other disappointed kite flyers gathered their limp string and broken kites and headed for their cars.

Eventually, a man with a battery-powered bullhorn announced the contest was finished. Officials awarded prizes for the most original, smallest, worst, or funniest kite, working their way to the best and highest-flying kite, which of course was the Shepard entry. Shep would always remember that prize: a bright red Eveready flashlight with two "D" batteries. Somehow it didn't seem appropriate, he thought then, in light of the great feat he had just performed. Shep was thinking of something more in line with a TV set, or a bicycle. Nonetheless, father and son were justifiably proud to return home with their winning kite and the First Place flashlight.

Throughout Shep's childhood and into adolescence, not a single kite-less spring went by.

Using the conservative three-stick design his father had passed on from his own kite-flying Depression days, Shep built a particularly unusual kite from foil-reinforced paper, constructing it in the alley behind The Prescott Courier newspaper office from which he daily delivered papers. The mother of some neighborhood children for whom Shep's mother babysat, had dropped off a box of supplies for an upcoming craft bazaar. In the box, Shep found a textile spool of silk thread so thin and strong that he felt as though it would cut his hand in half before it would break. With a large quantity of this very special thread and a gusty Saturday afternoon, Shep flew this small kite to such an altitude it could no longer be viewed by the naked eye.

Within an hour, first five, then ten of the neighborhood kids had gathered around to see this boy holding a spool of thread that ascended almost straight up into the sky and was attached to what seemed to be nothing. Each boy in turn would take the spool and feel the strong, steady tug of the kite somewhere in the upper stratosphere, just to know it was there.

Ultimately, the kite soared so high that Shep could not reel it in because of the multi-thousand-yard distance at which it was flying. After more than two hours, heat and moisture took its toll on the earthly paper kite and its string simply went slack in Shep's hands and he knew it had soared on without its tethering string. But judging from the direction it had been heading, Shep pictured it blowing and gliding, set free, finally floating to earth way beyond the small Arizona town where he lived. Perhaps it would eventually land somewhere far beyond Chino Valley -- thirteen miles to Prescott's north -- or maybe, he thought grandly, it would get as far as Canada.

Experimenting years later in another kite contest, the now-grown Shep would manage to split a very fine two-ply napkin apart and, using only one sheet and balsa wood struts, construct an Oriental two-stick kite that measured only three inches by four. He knew it was possible to make kites half or even a quarter that size, but that there was ultimately a dimension below which a kite could not be flown. In that contest years later in Colorado, Shep continuously flew the miniature kite on a delicate string of oriental silk thread to an altitude of twenty to thirty feet, winning first place among some seventy-five entries that ranged from amateur to experienced kite makers.

The spring breezes in San Francisco were no different than those at home and at the training school Shep planned to build another kite. He and Dave once again adjourned to the dusty shop in the evenings and built a large version of the famous three-stick design. Using heavy commercial butcher paper like his first kite, seamed with reinforcing tape and outer guy wires of heavy nylon cording, the two overlooked no detail as the monolithic kite with its seven-foot width took form -- except how to get it out of the boiler room door. Finally, on one particularly sunny and windy day, the two reluctantly broke the main crossbeam of the finished kite and wedged it through the doorway, where they splinted the beam back to its taut position. They nursed the huge kite up the three flights of winding stairs to the roof of the dorm building, and from that high vantage point attached it to a commercial reel of 60-pound twine and sent the behemoth toward the bright sky.

"Here, Dave, you take the first leg," Shep said, handing him leather workgloves to wear on his tender student hands.

It was magnificent to see, as Dave gently reeled it up. The pull was of such intensity they had to steady each other as the giant kite took to the sky. After a time of splendid flying, the boys took turns spinning it in, but they hadn't counted on the tremendous opposition of air-to-kite.

"I can't hold it anymore, Dave," Shep said. "Let's tie it to this handrail."

Time had flown by, metaphorically speaking, and class was calling.

"I don't want to leave it here unattended," Shep told Dave. "You get to class and I'll hang out here on the roof and watch it."

Since Shep's class was only a speed-reading lab, he planned to stay with the kite until the wind died down and he could retrieve it. Within ten minutes, however, the kite made a sweeping horizontal pass by the balcony before its elegant tail wrapped securely about the spire at the nearby St. Mary's Cathedral. People on the sidewalk saw the slack string dangling from roof to spire and knew at once where the crime had originated.

Inevitably, a disgruntled teacher appeared on the roof.

"Leave that blasted kite," he ordered, "and get to class."

Reluctantly, Shep abandoned the stranded kite.

The boys had rather a hard time explaining to the headmaster their illicit activity and its unexpected conclusion. Though done on free time, kite atrocities were nonetheless banned at the school in the future, and no doubt the Catholic Church's janitor grumbled as he ascended the sharp tower later to untangle the unseemly parasite from the chapel spire.

An unsightly end to a beautiful kite, Shep reflected, unaware that on his greatest adventure of all – a sojourn on the sea -- his kite flying mentality might be the thing that could turn the tides of danger in which he and Dave would find themselves so many years later.

Just then Shep's pleasant memory was rudely interrupted. Captain Dave was yelling something at him... *Oh yes, hoist the sails. We have wind astern!*

32
Bad Luck on Board

Old fishermen's superstitions recount that having clergy on board a ship is unlucky, as are women, black valises, umbrellas, or red-haired or cross-eyed persons. Even in these modern times of Global Positioning and sensitive Fathometer technology, some of the old beliefs still exist as bad omens, and ministers on board is one of them. Though Dave and Shep certainly pooh-poohed anything as silly as that, nonetheless, the two ministers encountered some terrible trouble on their crossing that could make a sane person wonder if the old superstitions weren't true.

Looking back at the night when the two friends had made their ocean-going plan, they had chosen an arbitrary date one year away. It would be May. That was the surest bet for a safe transpacific crossing, for of all twelve months, the fairest is always May. Unfortunately, the two were merely expeditionaries, not meteorologists, or they would have realized they'd unwittingly chosen -- yes, the best possible month -- but the worst possible year. Nineteen ninety-two was the year of El Nino, and when El Nino is present, all bets are off as to what conditions will prevail. Its warming of the waters creates various phenomena that affect tides, currents and barometric pressures -- in short, the stability of the ocean.

Unwittingly, the two had launched their journey into the jaws of one of the most treacherous storms of that summer season. Six months later on the Atlantic seaboard, six men would die on a swordfishing boat named the "Andrea Gail", in a maelstrom nicknamed "The Perfect Storm," in which El Nino was instrumental.

From their second day at sea, Dave had begun teaching Shep the regimen of chart keeping. Though not required for small craft, the record was indicative of seamanship at its highest level, and in this case, of the seaman who kept the record. Every waking hour on the hour during the sail, Dave would complete a metric chart, meticulously filling it in category by category with such information as the temperature of the water, the direction of the wind, the air temperature outside, the visibility, all the way up to and ending with measuring the barometric pressure.

Dutifully, Dave would stand on deck draped in an always sea-wet coat, clipboard in hand, feeling very nautical as he noted the exact time on his watch, the precise location on the compass, and filled in space after space of data with a Number 2 pencil. Unfortunately, none of this recordkeeping could prepare the men for what was eventually to come their way.

On the aft wall of the cabin just inside the gangway hung Mini's official barometer. Truth be known, however, it wasn't a real barometer. The men were traveling with such primitive equipment that they had instead substituted a used backpacker's altimeter. Not a terribly exact piece of equipment with its clock-like dial, it would nonetheless alert them to any change in air pressure. Numbers going up from zero meant high pressure, numbers dropping down from zero indicated low pressure, and so the altimeter would act as a moderately accurate barometer. Of all the things Shep learned early on in the trip and perhaps his fastest observation was that when the needle dropped below zero it meant foul weather and to Shep, knee-shaking terror.

In addition to the altimeter, the boat was equipped with a small battery-operated single frequency weather receiver common to some sailing vessels. This device allowed the men to receive one, and only one, message at the top of every hour. It was the National Weather Service's broadcast specifically for the area of reception, alerting sea-going vessels of pending weather conditions.

When turned on, the small receiver would hum and hiss with static until a single tone rang out. Immediately after the tone would be a very brief, almost robotic voice giving the next eight-hours' weather forecast. For whatever reason, Shep became utterly apprehensive of the sound of that tone, as he waited to hear its next prognostication. While Dave was always matter-of-fact, emitting a, "hmmm," or a, "well then," at the reports, Shep, who said nothing, felt he could better have expressed his feelings with a shriek. Even when the weather was perfect, he dreaded every turning of the hour, especially that bleak one just before midnight.

The men had set to sea knowing from journals they'd read that the first three hundred miles, known as the coastal waters, are always the most miserable part of the venture, so they'd expected to stay wet for the first three days and be somewhat cold and uncomfortable. The boat ride would also no doubt be bumpy and rough in comparison to the smooth sailing they could anticipate once they broke out of those waters.

But 1,400 miles later, when the barometer registered a drop and Mini hit a squall, which amounted to a mild gale, they were mildly perplexed, having no idea they were heading directly into the destructive path of Hurricane Andrew. With the first barometric dip, almost immediately everything took on a severe edge. The seas around them became turbulent, the skies dark and cloudy and a drizzling rain sprouted from the gloomy night. Dave and Shep buckled down to do what they could, which was to keep their watches and their charts.

By the third day, redemptively, the barometer climbed back up over a period of eight hours and the weather began to break up. Thinking the mild storm a fluke, the men were not prepared to see the barometer take a second dive, this time dropping lower in its descent than the first time. In the darkness of the cabin, Dave and Shep huddled knee to knee breathlessly listening to the small wall-mounted radio, waiting for the crisp tone of a report amidst the crackling. The dim glow of the 15-watt bulb overhead lit their nervous expressions.

Eventually, like an unwelcome harbinger of bad news, the tone did arrive, exactly on time, and the non-emotional voice of some functionary began to read the cards of their future.

The signs of immediate weather were all about them, clouds pulling and pushing against each other in the skies, masking any light from the celestial bodies above. The seas became angrier, the winds piped up.

"Let's reef the mainsail to less than a third," Dave ordered.

With lines taut and every contingency dealt with, the two continued upon a stormy sea, now in a three-quarter gale. The seas were running eighteen to twenty feet high with 45-knot winds. It occupied their keenest attention, and strangely enough the night seemed short with all there was to do.

The phrase, "Time stalked quickly by on velvet feet," popped into Shep's head, but he couldn't concentrate enough to remember if it was a poem or just something he'd made up.

The storm worsened. The crash of the sea against Mini's bow and over her top was not nearly as frightening as the sound of her straining against it. The feel of the sail pulling forward and then the sea pitching back against it gave a strange undulation to the ship's motion as it continued to sail into the teeth of the storm.

Fortified with full foul weather gear: so'easters, boots, and hands covered with gloves, the men gripped the sodden shrouds and adjusted the sails. Dave struggled across the deck, pulling in the ropes, kicking his lifeline out of the way to keep from getting tangled in it. All the way to the Mini's bow, he crawled and climbed, unjamming the roller-reefing mechanism before jumping with a thud to the cockpit floor and swinging around to take the helm.

Although distracted by the percussion of noise, they both saw that Mini had begun taking on substantial water. The hatches, which they'd sealed with foam gaskets, had begun to leak under the pressure and continuous pounding of the water over the bow. The ceiling in the cabin was dripping with water, saturating the cushions of both the V-berth and the starboard quarter-berth. Because of the predominantly southern direction Mini was heeling, one of the quarter berths carried the bulk of the water, while the portside temporarily stayed relatively dry. More and more water poured in, spilling into the gangway. Another hour and the entire inside of the cabin was as wet with the accumulation of water as the floor below. The hunter green carpet they'd installed for this voyage was now under an inch of water and slogged nastily underfoot.

Dave and Shep were forced to stay above board, sloshing about the cockpit, working the sails, or simply watching the maelstrom all around them. Taking turns at the wheel, they fought to keep Mini steering straight on into the waves as she fought back with an equal will to broach the waves at a sideways angle in what would mean a deadly welcome to Davy Jones' locker. Foam seethed on the crests of the now 40-foot waves, shot through with light before they hit Mini with cracks that sounded like gunshots. Nothing but sound boiled above and below the men, with the rumble of water, wind, and the machine they called Mini, all churning against each other.

Towards dawn of the fifth day, the barometer steadied and began to ascend towards normality. Although the seas were still tumbling, the men counted on the fact that the storm was over.

The sun over Friday's horizon revealed a sea covered with clouds for a hundred miles around. The wind was brisk but settling, and the seas seemed to want to rest.

"I don't get it," Dave pondered aloud. "To all indications things are looking better, but the weather report is calling for continued loss of barometric pressure."

"Since we don't know exactly where we are right now," Shep speculated, "maybe the broadcast is for a different area that could be hundreds of miles away."

They optimistically adopted this as their reality as they listened to the drone of the radio report every hour on the hour. The men were not surprised, however, when they heard no forecast for better weather. So, they spent their time re-checking the rigging, bailing the accumulated water, and mopping the cabin floor.

Dave had disconnected the self-steering vane during the storm to keep the pressure of the sea from pounding against the skeg rudder below Mini and breaking the small chains holding it together. Now, he reconnected it.

They continued to wring water out of the boat, pushing it forcibly through the scuppers, re-stowing jumbled equipment, pumping the bilge. But in the middle of these activities they noticed the barometer was taking a third plummet into the depths of its gauge. This time the pressure dropped so fast they could physically see the needle sweeping downwards. This sign was incomprehensible to the men. They looked out the portholes, then 360-degrees around at the sea from the cockpit. Seeing no black clouds, no raucous waves, they thought surely the bad weather must be over. But the renewed storm had yet to begin. By mid-morning they were toiling away again as the night before. Weary, but too nervous to eat or even relieve themselves, they pushed on in an adrenal emergency mode. With eyes wide and fists clenched, the two continued monitoring the sky and waves.

By afternoon the seas had once again risen to thirty-five feet with winds peaking at forty-five. They lowered the sails to a bare minimum and began to hand-sail Mini, taking turns at the helm, keeping their course and watching for rogue waves. Mini's bow would dive into the oncoming waves, then bounce back up time after time through the long afternoon and into the evening.

As the sun went down, the two fatigued men made no conversation, but spoke in low voices to themselves incessantly, each wondering what more they could do.

They watched the storm build fiercely around them. The barometer bottomed out and Dave and Shep realized they had entered into a full force gale for the first time in the past eight days. By midnight the waves were exploding around them.

They knew all too well that any wave tumbling over the boat from behind would breach their stern and send them under. Their single goal became to face the waves head on, taking them at an angle off the bow, swinging the boat around if need be when the seas shifted. They watched vigilantly to prevent the knockdown the sea would bring if Mini ceased to meet the waves front on. For hours, the boat continued dodging and weaving through the angry seas.

By 2 a.m., the men were wringing wet and exhausted. The boat was rocking ferociously from side to side and up and down. Both Dave and Shep were plagued with vertigo. Nothing seemed quite right. The compass was no longer of value because they had no course in such a storm. No stars were visible through the heavy clouds. The men were locked in a giant canyon of sound with the ocean roaring about them and Mini cracking and moaning her discomfort.

The two moved as if in a slow motion movie sequence, no longer able to physically cope with the reeling ship and sea. Knowing which way to steer became as confusing as finding the door in a carnival Fun House. Time and again the waves crashed down, hitting the men with stunning blows on the head and shoulders. Though unhurt, they were demoralized, feeling as if the sea itself was letting them know who carried the muscle.

They could not know it then, but somewhere near them in the self-same storm, a 50-foot Ferro-cement sailing vessel sheared a mast. As the giant pole fell, it severely injured one of the five crewmembers. Calling for help on their superior GPS and radio equipment, the Coast Guard rescued them at sea. Though unaware of that crisis, Dave and Shep *did* know that were Mini to capsize or become incapacitated, she would be an unknown cipher in the sea. They would be unable to call for help and their whereabouts would never be known. They were on their own.

Drenched, Dave couldn't help but think of this as a water baptism. Ironically, that had been his big contention with the Salvation Army. It was the reason he left, striking out on his evangelical own and founding his own congregation.

He had been baptized in a river in a ceremony of tremendous spiritual significance to him, and yet the Salvation Army believed in baptism as only symbolic, not a ritual of any importance. To Dave, it was so much more. Not excluded in his passion for water baptism was his love of the ocean. The symbolism of water itself was strong and enduring in Dave's mind and heart, so the power of this ocean baptism was not lost on him.

Eventually, the man off watch had to lock the cabin to keep the wild water out, while the man in the cockpit stood in rushing water, clamped to the floor by his lifeline. As they changed shifts, the man going to the cabin felt keen guilt at taking his place below knowing the other man must stand in his stead above in the bristling brine.

The winds rose to such a fierce velocity that the entire boat shuddered from stem to stern. It was impossible to tell if Mini was moving. As if in a trance, the two men felt the wind passing over the shrouds and stick.

Shep couldn't finish his two-hour shift at 2 a.m. Within an hour, he banged on the cabin door and called for Dave, who was now lying in a six-inch-deep trough of water. As he pulled himself up towards Shep, his rope still attached and leading out to deck, Shep grabbed him by the shoulder and pulled him the rest of the way up.

"I can't stay out any longer," Shep yelled apologetically over the din.

"That's okay, you go on down, I'll take it from here," Dave yelled back, and grasped the quivering helm.

Below, Shep lay down in the cold seawater and pulled a soaked army blanket over his chest. The damp warmth of his breath moving in and out served as the only heat. Huge waves flung the boat from side to side as he jammed himself between the berths and braced his shoulders in the passageway. Hearing the cracking sounds of wood and fiberglass above, Shep felt like a man edging himself into his own coffin.

In fear, he yelled out, "Are you there, Dave?"

Amid the deafening roar, he heard Dave stomp his

boot hard above and answer, "I'm here."

Shep remembered another dark night, the darkest of his life next to the unknown he was now experiencing, and he knew that like that other time, he was with the one man who could get him through it, save God himself.

33
Death Comes to Call

It had been a typical spring evening at Officers' Training with the students confined to their quarters after dinner for two hours' enforced study time without music or distraction of any kind and with no access to any part of the building except the library for research. It was then that students customarily wrote research papers, read assignments, or studied for exams. Then, at 7:30 p.m., they metamorphosed at some unheard signal in the air that let them know study hour was finished. The young men donned ball caps and tennis shoes and walked about freely, knowing they could stay up till curfew at 9. They still had time to make a run to the nearby convenience store, or even other destinations, if they had a pass.

This particular day was April Fools, 1974, and Shep and his girlfriend, Debby, and another couple, Tom Rainwater and Linda Story, decided to take a stroll to the Mayfair Market, just down the road. They headed off shortly after the liberating hour. Tom and Linda hesitated at the traffic light while it changed, then continued through the intersection. Just as Shep and Debby were about to follow, a fellow student leaned from an upper window and called down, "Hey, bring me a snack?"

"Sure," Shep called back. "You can pay me later."

"No, here's the cash," the young man answered, tossing some coins down, the last of which Shep missed and stooped to gather up.

Life would spin on the circuit of those coins. It was the defining moment that would alter two men's lives, inexplicably sparing one and sending the other to his death.

The light changed again, and Shep and Debby hurried across to catch up with Tom and Linda. At mid-street, through some light San Francisco fog, the visage of a man materialized as he walked past them, a light-skinned Black man with a red tint to his hair, freckles sprayed across his nose, yellow sunglasses for seeing at night, and wearing an olive drab raincoat. Shep noticed his hands were clenched. The two men's eyes met and they seemed to almost hesitate in passing, that moment somehow frozen between them. Then they moved on. Shep stepped onto the far curb -- a step into a different future. Walking a few more paces he saw a man's body lying in his path. It was the body of his friend, Tom Rainwater, though Shep didn't recognize him in death. It looked like no one he knew, just a man. Hearing struggling and weeping at the edge of traffic, Shep looked over to see Linda bleeding, kneeling in the road and curled into a fetal position with her back arched like a cat, trying to hold herself close. Confused, Shep walked toward her.

A plainclothes policeman appeared from seemingly nowhere with a camera and a briefcase like in some surrealistic crime thriller. Running toward Shep, he shouted, "Get back. I'm a police officer."

Shep stepped away, then looked back again at

Tom, still not registering who that man was and that he was dead. He turned back to the officer who was bending over Linda's moaning form.

"I know her," Shep told the cop. "It's Linda Story."

Then turning in a daze, he grasped Debby's hand and they ran back toward the school, up the stairs, and pounded heavily on a female officer's door.

"What is it, Michael?" she asked, opening the door and looking puzzled.

Shep could hardly speak, his breath rasping hard and fast.

"Linda has been shot. She's lying in the street," he said, pointing vaguely.

The blood drained from the officer's face.

"Where's Tom?" she asked, knowing Linda and Tom were inseparable.

At that moment, something snapped in Shep's mind and he realized the unfathomable.

"Tom is dead."

Within mere minutes, it seemed, the Salvation Army cadets began straggling into the chapel, spreading the news among themselves that their classmate was dead and Linda in the hospital, her condition unknown. They shed tears, whispered prayers, then dispersed to their rooms for a sleepless night to assimilate the terrible events, comforted only with a promised report come morning -- all but one. Shep could not go to his room, could not go into the dark, could not be alone. In a state of utter terror, quaking, he sat hunched in the hallway under the bare lights, staring blankly at the far wall.

Dave came. He sat across from Shep like a bridge, his feet pressed against Shep's feet. He stayed through that interminable night. Never sleeping; in a vigil of comfort, speaking of Tom -- who was Dave's roommate -- telling Shep things he had not previously known about his friend Tom.

The greatest comfort Shep took that night was not in the ethereal thought that a great God he knew was personally over all, but that Dave, his friend, a strong man, was with him.

It would come out eventually that Tom was one of sixteen random people murdered by one of the most radical sects operating in the Fillmore District. Called, "Death Angels," by themselves; "The Zebra Killers," by the investigating police, they were from the Nation of Islam temple, the same one from which Dave and Shep had been turned away that Saturday evening not so long ago. Back then, they'd had no way of knowing that the pseudo-Islamic teachings of the Death Angels presented that Whites were not human beings, but "blue-eyed devils," "white devils," and "grafted snakes."

Linda would recover from her injuries, and Shep and Debby would testify at the killer's trial, for which he would receive only fourteen years in prison.

At Tom's funeral some days later, attended by both cadets and officers, a cadre of San Francisco law enforcement, and half the city it seemed, Dave and Shep walked arm-in-arm to say farewell to their friend.

"I'll meet you at the Gates," Dave whispered to Tom in his casket.

34

Disastrous Neptune

A monstrous wave broke over Mini, pouring through the hatch and down the walls, trickling inside the windows and turning Shep from thoughts of his own survival. He was immediately fearful that Dave would be swept away above. Unable to think, or sleep, or stay below, he stepped toward the hatch, then hesitated. Reaching into the cubby above his head, he felt for the plastic of his California driver's license. Locating it by feel in the dark, he carefully tucked it into his boot…just in case. Just in case he didn't make it through this storm. If his body was ever found, at least they'd know who he was. Then Shep climbed out, pushing the hatch open and dropping it into the lower cabin behind him.

Neither man could keep an hour watch anymore.

"We're too far gone," Shep cupped his hands and yelled at Dave.

"How about this," Dave hollered back above the noise. "We keep our ropes on, stay hooked together, and just go up and down, ten minutes on, ten minutes off?"

"Right," Shep replied.

At 3:30 a.m., they began 10-minute watches. At 3:40, Dave took the helm. At 3:50, Shep replaced him, and so on through the night. As one man would go below, fall into the brine and close his eyes to shut out the sight of the surging sea, the other man would brace his body in the cockpit with both hands on the tiller and watch for any treacherous sea that could sneak up from behind.

After four or five trades at the helm, Dave took over.

"I'm going to stay for twenty," he told Shep. "Take some rest."

After swinging down below and collapsing on the floor, Shep became almost immediately immersed in a dark and murky sleep. No sooner did he find that quiet place than Dave called, "You're on."

"I'm good," Shep groggily lied. "I'll take it. You sleep."

Three more trades. The two agonized to see the other's pain, each quietly giving the other another ten minutes. The only contest became who could stretch time the furthest on their watch.

The storm continued to rage in a fury that could get no worse, and the men faced the fact that they were truly in the most menacing situation they could have imagined in their worst nightmares. The eternal optimist, however, Dave saw this terrible storm as merely a temporary setback on the journey to Hawaii. Shep was not at all sure this wasn't the end.

By dawn, they were busy keeping Mini afloat. The cabin was trashed, with provisions dislodged, or broken, and mingled with salt water, a catastrophe the men ignored, their full attention riveted to the ongoing storm.

Noon Saturday approached. Both kept to deck, pumping water, re-securing ropes and lines, keeping the sails tight and trim, but nothing changed. The storm had become so severe the boat would no longer operate. Any slice of sail was too much cloth. The winds were gusting upwards of sixty miles an hour. With just the bare mast aloft the boat sped on at four knots.

The storm was also fearlessly fickle. It constantly shifted direction making it impossible for the men to plot a reasonable course on the undulating water trap. In desperation they deployed the sea anchor, a heavy canvas drogue that Shep had carefully folded and stowed under Dave's tutelage the night before they'd left. Dave had assured him they would never have use for it on this voyage. Theoretically, this device would stop Mini from rolling down the sheer walls of water that continued to pick up from the bottom of every trough. They hoped that by dropping this underwater parachute into the frothing depths, Mini's stern would be dragged in the direction of the following seas and prevented from tumbling end over end as she descended the steep cliffs of water.

Seeing Dave fighting to deploy the drogue on its heavy lines, Shep struggled across the deck to help him fasten the bitter ends of the ropes to two beefy stern cleats. They watched the bright yellow apparatus go deep, sinking under the waves and flopping away from them, and felt a corresponding lightness in their stomachs as the boat skid roller-coaster-like into a sliding drop to the bottom of the next trough. The ocean instantly bounced Mini back up the spine of the next wave, the G-forces shearing the skin back on the men's cheeks as the boat sprang into open air.

The drogue finally opened under water, the force of its pull against Mini's stern yanking with fearsome power. The little boat about-faced to the running sea then stopped, fell forward, and caught her chin on the lowers of the next trough. The drogue lines tangled. Yanking on the ropes and trying to unfoul it, the men floundered as the sea set up the next terror-filled carnival ride. With seas still standing steeply at sixty feet, the spray off the tops of the waves was like standing in a continuous downpour without a drop of rain in sight.

Mini shuddered as the underwater parachute struggled some twenty yards off the stern with the men attempting to correct it again and again. Suddenly, its ropes pulled tight and again the men felt the entire weight of the ship hang by the two cleats as it shot the falls of the next wave that roared like Niagara beneath the boat. Mini evened out as the drogue heaved her back. Once again, the yellow parachute collapsed and Mini cut loose to spin perilously sideways, wagging loosely against the helm. Dave brought her about again, just as a monstrous wave crashed to the bow.

"I don't know what's wrong with this thing," Dave shouted. "It worked so perfectly at the boat show," he said, attempting some of his usually present good humor. Then on a sterner note, he added, "I don't think this thing can work, Shep. The seas are running too crazily."

In abject denial, Shep reassured him, "Oh no, it'll work. That's what it's designed to do."

"Shep. It *isn't* going to work," Dave replied, his bloodshot eyes registering regret.

"What's that supposed to mean?" Shep said, staring steadily at Dave, who was standing knee-deep in water and looking *up* at the ocean instead of out.

Without a shred of humor or sarcasm, Dave looked at Shep and said, "It means we may see God today."

At that moment the thought crossed Dave's

stunned mind that he couldn't possibly have known when he learned to sail as a boy of eight on the lake that fronted his house in Spokane, that this is where sailing would lead him. As he clumsily struggled to master the art of sailing the eight-foot El Toro dinghy his father had taken for a debt on unpaid-for Pella windows, who would have thought that this wonderful new adventure he so loved would bring him to the edge of death and beyond. The irony did not escape him that the very thing that had brought him through his parent's divorce would eventually kill him. That the ocean in front of which he'd fallen to his knees at fifteen -- that magnificent ocean before which he'd wept to see its beauty -- would be the last thing he would see on this earth. Not the loving face of his wife, or those of his sons, but the ocean -- the wondrous, magical ocean for which he yearned like a lover.

For the next few minutes the roar of the sea, the lift of the waves, all seemed to go silent, unreeling in slow motion as the two contemplated their probable fate. Without another word, they turned back to their work, continuing to hold true to the lines and dodge the waves.

Dave began pulling in the drogue rope. Shep grabbed onto the rope from behind to help bring in the heavy sea anchor. Lightning flashed, reflecting in the glass face of Dave's diving watch, a Seiko that Shep had given him as they began their journey. On its back he'd had it engraved, "To my seaworthy friend."

His thoughts were interrupted as the gale drove another half-dozen waves in succession into the bow with a force that surely felt like head-on collisions would at seventy miles an hour.

Pitching his head to the side near Shep's face,

Dave yelled through the storm, "I'm sorry I got you into this, Shep."

As though arguing above the noise, Shep yelled back without anger, "Whaddya mean? I'm the one who suggested we take this trip. I'm the one that got us into this."

With real anger then, Dave faced him and shouted back, "Yes, but *you* didn't know what could happen. I've always known this was how it could be. We may not make our way out of this, Shep. I would gladly give my life to keep you alive, but I don't know how."

"That won't happen," Shep replied defiantly. "If I drown, I'll be holding your head out of the water when I do."

In a voice drained of emotion, but with finality, Dave said, "It's time for us to go below, Shep. I'm putting the ship into heave-tow position."

"Why?" Shep persisted, grabbing a winch handle for support against the wind.

Swinging around to face him, Dave shouted back, "We're lashing the rudder to port. We're going down below and hope she doesn't roll. We're going to put our feet on the ceiling and let the sea have her way...whatever that is."

With foam swirling around his legs and salt brine hitting him in the face, Shep refused to believe that Dave was saying what he was saying.

"No. We can't do this. I'm not going down."

"You won't last an hour up here, Shep," Dave said, wading resolutely toward the cabin.

Watching the retreat of Dave's solid back, Shep realized with a start that Dave was far less afraid to die than he. Perhaps Shep had seen Death at closer quarters than Dave. Not once, but twice he'd heard the Reaper call his name and miss. Eighteen years ago, when Tom was shot, Shep had escaped dying by a trigger's hair, but before that, when he was eighteen years old, Shep had felt what it would be like to die.

He'd gone to visit a girlfriend on Mount Vernon Street in Prescott, driving his souped-up, shiny cream-colored Volkswagen "Bug" of which he was most proud.

Young, careless, in a hurry, Shep had swung the Bug in a U-turn in the middle of the street, not looking for oncoming traffic. As fate or bad luck would have it, a dump truck with a full load of rocks and dirt was barreling down the tree-lined street toward him, laying on its brakes and horn. Shep would remember nothing of the ensuing accident; only feel the hair on the back of his neck raise for the rest of his life whenever he heard the squealing of brakes.

He would wake three weeks later from a coma, much to the surprise of his family, friends and mother -- who'd cleaned his Sunday suit for his funeral -- with a mending pelvis, a still-healing arm where the gearshift had punched through it, and the back of his head full of scars so deep it looked as if he'd been attacked by a cutlass. So yes, Shep knew the smell of Death's sweet and terrible breath and he wanted nothing to do with it.

Though he had no way of knowing this, thousands of miles across the ocean, back in his small hometown of Prescott, Arizona, his Aunt Lola Moreno awoke at this very moment. Sitting bolt upright in bed, she shook her husband Ascension awake.

"Chon, get up. Michael is in terrible danger," she said.

Swinging her feet onto the cold floor, she shuffled

into the kitchen to find a candle and match.

"We must pray for him," she said, as she began fingering the worn brown wood of her rosary beads.

As the starboard sea rolled once again across the cabin, Shep begged, "C'mon Dave, there's gotta be some way out of here. Please. Please don't leave me."

Yelling back with sad eyes, Dave reiterated, "There's nothing more we can do, Shep. We can't put up any canvas; the wind will tear it off. We can't steer the ship over bounce and foam, so the sea drogue is worthless. That's it. That's all there is. We've done all the steps."

His mind churning like the ocean around him, Dave believed that they'd be safest in the cabin. He wasn't giving up, just accepting what might happen and giving he and Shep the best way to survive that he knew. He had no way of knowing that in Shep's mind, the cabin would be as dangerous a place as being thrashed by the raging water. Recalling all the cans and pans and odd assortment of things in the cabin, Shep could only imagine that they'd be pummeled to death by the lethal tossing about of the loose detritus inside that enclosed space.

In the vacuum of the moment, it seemed to Dave there *were* only two heartbeats on the entire ocean and that those were surely only one heartbeat away from their maker. He wasn't afraid. He was ready to die, if that was what was going to happen. For all the problems his parents had, they'd taught him that he should never be afraid of failure. Sometimes, no matter how hard you try, some things will simply not work out. Eva, too, had known the possibility that Dave would not return when she sent him off.

"You're both ready to meet God, if that's what happens," she'd told Dave the night before he left. "I love you more than you can know, but if God wants you, then you're ready. 'Let Go and Let God.'"

Dave really hadn't believed he and Shep would die on this journey. The weather was forecast to be good, the ship was in perfect shape. But then again, you never knew. It was against that possibility that Dave had made videos for each of his boys before he left. Just in case. Eva had them in safekeeping and if Dave made it home, Hans and Ben would never see those videos of their father telling them how much he loved them and admonishing them to care for their mother in his absence and to grow up to be fine men.

As though deaf in a talking movie, Shep stood dumbstruck in the silence of his own fear as another sledgehammer blow struck the boat. Then, in a human being's most acute desperation, he remembered the small sail Dave had shown him before the trip. It was for storm sailing only. Triangular and no more than twenty-eight inches clew to clew, the small jib resembled more a bulky piece of rug than a sail. Thicker than a doormat, but made of canvas, imbedded in each corner of the sail was a heavy brass grommet meant to take the heaviest of all shackles. It seemed to Shep, the flier of kites, that it was almost like a small kite in its triangular configuration. Perhaps that's why he thought of it.

"Couldn't we fly the storm jib off the bow and let it pull us?" he shouted toward Dave, as another wave pitched the tiny ship forward, leaning the mast at a 45-degree angle to the clouded sky and rocking both men and boat down once again to slam into the bowels of the next wave. "Can't we just put this one sail up and try?"

"In this wind?! The bare stick is almost heeling us out," Dave yelled.

"Please. Dave. What do we have to lose? I'm just not ready to meet you at the Gates."

Flashing unbidden through Dave's mind was the passage from "Prayers of the Sea":

The sea is so large and our boat is so small. Lead us to port.

Stepping forward and grabbing the top of the hatch, Dave lifted it a foot, hesitated, then pushed it back to closed position. He turned and shouted in resignation, "Okay. We'll latch up the storm jib and we'll see."

Within minutes, Shep was up front riding the boat like it was a mechanical bull, hooking up what they hoped would be a miracle. With winds stiff as frozen sheets, it took only moments after securing the third clew of the jib before they got their answer. Holding to the bare mast, Shep looked back at Dave, dark waves a backdrop behind him, and felt the boat tug to starboard. Grabbing the helm and straining backwards to get the boat to cooperate, Dave looked more oarsman than skipper. Sculling the helm like an oar, he wrenched it to starboard. Mini began to strain at hull speed and the momentum shifted. With a slight hesitation, she swung into place.

Astonished, Dave hollered, "She's answering the helm! Racket that jib in tighter and secure the lines."

Dave inched the boat up the face of another colossal wave, cresting the top without changing angles or direction, and slid her smoothly down the other side, the tiny storm jib straining under the weight of the wind. Still riding low in the water from remaining provisions and having taken on water as well, Mini's small body was buried deep into the ocean with almost no freeboard visible. Miraculously, her submarine-like positioning seemed to hold her into the side of the waves as she climbed, as if the suction of the water itself hugged her hull to the seas as the boat ascended and descended at impossibly acute angles.

The hours crawled by and the men gained confidence. Standing side by side they shifted positions to hold the helm as the angry seas continued to swirl in and around the cockpit, no longer seeming so chilling or so deadly.

An interminable time later, Dave shouted, "If this is the way it's going to be for the next 1,000 miles, we'll stay the course."

With the most courageous affirmation he could dig up, Shep replied, "Aye, aye, skipper," and made his way below.

It would be another forty-eight hours before the direness of such a close call would hit Dave, and like a time-lapse photo he would find himself shaking uncontrollably and crying alone on his 2 a.m. watch.

35

Lost in Limbo

Discovering themselves still alive at dawn, the two waterlogged men were incredulous. As a sort of celebration and healing, Dave resurrected the old jury-rigged stove and lit a fire from a bundle of greasewood sticks, then began burning everything he could find, including a wooden crate of half-spent provisions ruined in the storm. The soggy cabin cushions found places of honor around the hot fire. Dave also rounded up two apples. A suitable toast to life, he decided. Handing Shep one rosy orb and keeping the other for himself, the two chomped gratefully into the white flesh and gazed at the crackling fire that cast its amber glow on the cabin's ceiling. Its heat warming not only their long-cold limbs, but their hearts, as well, as they gazed upon the other -- their friend, their comrade -- and rejoiced in another day of life.

Stepping into the cockpit and holding onto the back stay, Dave loosened his foul-weather gear and whizzed joyfully into the sea, all the while singing, "Born Free," at the top of his happy lungs.

The men slowly regained their strength and bearings, having survived they hoped, the darkest part of their journey. The seas began to calm, though not quickly. The skies remained overcast and rolling in dark cloud for a hundred miles in every direction. Mini still bobbed like an insignificant cork on a vast pond as Dave cautiously advanced more and more sailcloth from the original storm jib; first to a small reefed-up main, to a partial jib, then to a half jib, half main, and finally set the main jib back in order.

The sailing was going well, but Dave had a larger problem. He was unable to site their location.

The storm had blown Mini well into the route toward Hawaii, he thought, but he didn't exactly know where they were. A few times when the skies would break, Dave would dash up to the deck, position himself with the sextant and go about the task of getting a fix as to their exact location. Shep would set the second hand of his watch, and with metronomic precision the two would check and quickly write down a series of numbers coding their position. Dave would then go below to wrestle with the charts and slide rules to interpret their sightings. Slowly, he began to realize there were conflicts from one stolen sighting to the next, as all the while they traveled under troubled skies. It became clear to him that, although not certain, it was possible they had been whisked on the current so far from the course they believed they were on that they may actually be out of the pocket of navigation for a directional fix. Dave began to speculate that he may indeed be starting with incorrect numbers and sabotaging his own calculations. He simply had to have realistic coordinates before he could find their exact location.

The best Shep could do was be supportive of Dave as he performed the tedious task of calculating position.

In his heart, Shep wished he could somehow carry his half of this portion of the responsibility. As another day and evening melted away, it was evident that Dave was more and more concerned about the lack of good, clear results for his celestial navigation.

"I just don't know where we are, Shep," he said. "I just don't know. Our calculations show us to be approximately 1,700 miles southwest of our departure."

The storm that had threatened their lives seemed to have actually tossed them miles ahead of schedule, but they couldn't be sure.

Too worried to sleep, the men aborted the usual routine of Shep on first watch and Dave below sleeping and both remained awake through the first watch and into the second. Shep reclined on the port aft of the quarter-berth as Dave leaned forward on the V-berth, and the two friends distracted themselves by remembering and chuckling about past escapades. Aware they were sailing in uncertainty until the sun could break through and provide them with a clearer picture, the men somehow felt it would be alright to ignore that fact, and without saying so, they simply left that subject outside the cabin for the night.

Shortly after 11 p.m., peering through the window with absolutely nothing to look at, Shep listened with one ear to Dave talking and with the other to the ceaseless sound of the water combing under the hull. Staring into the blackness in an easterly direction, for a split second he thought he saw a flash of light. Just as quickly, it vanished. Dave continued talking as Shep strained with his farthest stare, searching for that slight light he was sure he'd seen. As Dave paused for a breath, Shep said, "I've just seen something."

"There's nothing out there, Shep," Dave replied.

"Well, that big nothing has a light on it," Shep grinned.

Dave slid the small homemade curtains aside that half obstructed his portal view and he, too, pressed his nose to the Lexan window. Both men stared long and hard into the dark. Shep slid open the hatch and stuck his head out. Dave moved closer to Shep's port. On the slow and gentle seas, the men waited for the rise of their boat to meet that split second when perhaps the mast light on some elusive vessel might appear. Ten minutes, nothing. Twelve minutes, nothing.

"Are you sure you didn't just imagine it?" Dave asked.

"No. I was just looking into the darkness and there it was for a second. There's a ship out there somewhere."

Dave put his legs down and slid to the far berth, pushed a button, turned a knob, then keyed the radio microphone and called out, "Any vessel. Any vessel. This is the California sailing ship, Mini. Please reply."

As he adjusted the squelch on the radio, the high-pitched humming ceased, followed by dead silence. Keying again and with his best voice, Dave repeated the call slower and with more conviction, "Any vessel…."

For a moment the men's pulses picked up with hope. They said nothing, but the waiting took on a vibrant life of its own. The unspoken agreement between them was that it would be great to hear from anyone at this point.

Realizing that at night they would have the greatest potential for being heard, Dave matter-of-factly clipped the microphone back on its stanchion, but left the radio on. Two things were clear, Shep was not going up top to finish the second half of his watch, and Dave was not going to sleep, at least not yet. The two resumed their chat, both listening with half an ear to the ocean sliding around them on both sides, but the winds were steady and the boat continued to move farther and farther from the sighting.

"You know we have about a one-in-a-million chance of catching a ship in this area," Dave said. "First, we're not in a shipping lane, and second, if there was a ship nearby, it would most likely not see or hear us."

Cliché that it was, the men and the phantom boat were indeed, ships passing in the night. Almost half-an-hour passed and Dave readied to kill the radio to salt away the small portion of solar saved up for an emergency. It would be comforting to leave it on, just to make them feel better, but the electricity was more precious than the assurance.

As Dave reached to shut down the plant, it screeched to life. A voice tore through the radio in an accent that would be familiar only to people of Bombay, and some merchant marine called out, "Hello, hello? Vessel Mini? This is the Cyprian cargo ship...."

It was a vessel from Cyprus on channel VHS 16.

Keying the microphone, Dave responded, "Yes. We are enroute to Hawaii. Have been in a storm for some eight days and are without proper global positioning. Can you please tell us your location at this moment so we can find ourselves on our chart?"

The Indian sailor replied, "Most assuredly, we will help you. Please be waiting."

The men trembled with the thought that the ship could steam beyond their small radio reach in those lapsed moments or some other problem could suddenly cut them off. They counted the seconds, unconsciously holding their breath. In a relatively short time, which nonetheless seemed interminable, someone fed the positions to the seaman who was neither navigator or radio operator, and he, with his Gunga Din accent began to relate to the men Mini's current position.

"You are at latitude 28 and longitude 140, south by southwest..." and the signal began to break up, leaving no time for conversation, only the precious coordinates and the men's swift and sincere thank you to the great lumbering Greek ship. Dave clicked off the radio.

The men's minds contemplated the fact that their new friends didn't even know what their boat looked like, nor they theirs. Dave and Shep didn't know what that ship was carrying or where it was headed. Surely it must be to the Panama Canal, they thought, but they never got an answer to their questions. Strangely enough, in just that one small moment some poor man who no doubt worked way too hard for what he was given in return, had possibly saved their lives -- lives endangered for the second time in as many days. The two men thankfully never had to know what might have happened had they not been given some point of correction off which to reconcile all the distance the storm had forced upon them.

"I wonder why it took so long for someone to answer our call?" Shep speculated, conjuring up all kinds of imaginary ideas, including that they were in the midst of a mutiny and the two men had interrupted it. But the likely truth was that a late-night radio operator sitting with only a strong cup of coffee and a half-burned cigarette for company had heard a possible distress call, but was perhaps not conversant in English and had to summon someone who was, because universal maritime law dictates that no ship whatsoever shall ever turn away from any hailing by another vessel, especially if the crew might be in trouble. On a large sailing vessel, the crew is composed of many ethnicities, and on any given voyage dozens of languages are spoken. Without a doubt, some crewman was rousted from his night slumbers and rushed to the radio room where he sat down and talked to a lonely ship somewhere close by and inquired as to its welfare.

Throughout centuries of sailing those in distress have always known that if no other boat is nearby, you face fierce Neptune alone, but if any ship is within the range of voice or radio, it will abandon its course if need be and rush to your side.

The navigations are a great blessing to us, Shep wrote in his log.

It was a critical moment, like finding the key to the castle door and escaping the dungeon and dragon.

As it turned out, the men weren't as far afield as they thought they could have been, but without accurate coordinates they could have wandered untold days trying to rejoin their plotted course.

The winds picked up, and with directions now confirmed, the men began sailing swiftly toward their goal again. Mini faced straight into the wind and suffered teeth-chattering chop, but made a hundred miles a day.

⚓

May 16th -- This morning, while rinsing a spoon over the side of Mini, I saw a fish, black-and-white-striped, about fourteen inches long. It's some kind of pilot fish. He appears to be staying beside the boat, just beneath the bow. The little fellow isn't scared by the movement of my hand in the water, though he won't get closer than three or four feet, Shep wrote.

The men peered at their new companion from inches away. The fish moved neither forward or aft of the boat, but maintained his heading. Mini was doing six knots, but the small fish swam along handsomely. Evening came. The fish was still there, staying at the bow, but circling every few minutes. He seemed to be patrolling to make sure no other fish were about, though this portion of ocean was so unpopulated, the men couldn't imagine he'd have any competition.

Mini was compelled to change course to rest the steering vane. The fish followed suit, or more accurately it seemed, led the boat. No matter how the boat turned, the fish stayed as close as a button on a shirt. If Mini picked up speed from the passing force of a zephyr creeping across her path, the fish picked up his tempo. As the men and boat slowed to a crawl, the fish parked and rested beneath the bow.

For a hundred miles -- through one complete turn of the earth -- the little Titan hung with the men. Shep tossed cheese and peas toward him, but if not close enough for the fish to grab while on his course, he would refuse to move from his position. Several times the tidbits landed close enough to his chosen path that he ate them.

Trying carefully not to disturb the tiny guide, the men watched him for hours in utter fascination. To gauge his reaction, Shep tossed small pieces of wadded paper ahead of the boat, where they would land six-to-eight feet ahead. At the boat's speed, the objects came crashing toward the fish, where he would attack, let them slide by along Mini's girth, then carry on. Unfortunately, the Sunday night passage was very difficult, with Mini zigging and zagging through the night. By morning, the little pilot fish had fallen away. Perhaps being black-hulled, the fish had thought Mini was a migrating whale that would offer protection and food for a small guide. Whatever its motivation, the men missed its faithful steerage.

36

Burial at Sea

Had there been anyone to observe the two men so far in the middle of nowhere, they would not have been surprised to see the two ministers-at-sea conducting something of a service. But as it was, the audience was non-existent. The appointed leader of the day would select some readings, maybe strum a tune with no need for a hymnal, or sing some of the great hymns of the ages...and why not? The men knew them all by heart.

Day after day, during their small makeshift services, Shep would produce the old tome, "Prayers at Sea," by Capt. Joseph Parker. It was printed, they were surprised to see, in 1953, the year the two were born.

At the end of the third week, as Dave checked the charts one sunny morning, he realized they were dead over the Molokai channel of the Pacific, undoubtedly one of the deepest parts of the Pacific Ocean with a depth of three miles. At approximately 16,000 feet deep, the heaviest of steel compresses and ultimate darkness reigns. Having somehow endured the longer portion of the sabbatical in the irons of the doldrums, then having suffered the life-threatening tempest, and now being in the deepest part of the known ocean, the two decided they would observe a burial at sea. In the aftermath of the storm, and having re-digested what had taken place a week earlier, they realized they were not living on borrowed time, but rather were alive because of some special allowed passage.

"We've seen into the jaws of death, that's for sure, Shep…closer than we may again until our judgment day," Dave said, his face serious.

As they spoke of the meaning of this in the wee hours and on their watches, it seemed as though they surely must return as better men than they had departed. If that were not the case, this journey would boil down to no more than a long and arduous trip with an unanticipated element of danger.

"Maybe we should have a ceremony, Dave. We've survived an incredible event, just one more chapter in our lives as friends," Shep said. "But we've obviously been saved for some reason. Let's leave the worst of ourselves behind in a ceremony."

Shep thumbed through the small readings from the prayer book, and found a very solemn section, which had been used from the days of the first organized navies. Because men of the sea are rightfully committed back to its depths upon death, the burial at sea, while macabre to land folk, is an esteemed honor paid to a fallen sailor.

Dave and Shep thus determined that the only way to have a burial at sea when they were both so alive and thankfully so, would be to build effigies of themselves. So, throughout that day and into the late afternoon, the two men symbolically submitted their old lives, pre-voyage, to the past.

They built effigies of themselves from two planks of plywood that had been stored flat atop other supplies below the cabin floor hatch covers and brought along in case a repair would require a large piece of laminate material. With coping saws and hand-bits, the two men each traced their own form carefully on the face of the planking. Using knees for sawhorses and arms as braces, each cut two-foot miniature silhouettes of themselves from head to foot. When the outlines were sawn through, they used rasps and sandpaper to smooth the edges.

Before the official Burial at Sea each in turn, without consulting the other, slipped into the cabin and put on better clothes: a shirt with perhaps less streaks of salt, or a fresh pair of socks. They combed their hair to neatness and smoothed their beards as if going to a funeral.

The afternoon was still bright as they finished preparations for the funerals. Shep set out the prayer book. The wooden effigies of the men to be committed leaned bravely against the cabin. With true transparency, and with no one but God and themselves as witness, Dave and Shep sat knee-to-knee in the small cockpit and with indelible markers from the chart shelf slowly wrote upon the images of themselves the most grievous sins they'd ever committed, their deepest disappointments, their most horrendous failures.

An hour or more crept past as the two silently inscribed all the things each wished had never been written into the pages of their lives. Then, they who were not Catholics, in whispered tones confessed to the man of the cloth sitting across from them.

Having done this, they fashioned nooses with the skill of two boson mates, ornate and fancy with twisted knots, and slipped them over the plywood necks. Looping a double sheepshank on the other end, they passed it through the heavy eyelet of a fishing weight, four to five ounces each. Balancing the two at the edge of Mini's portside, Dave took the prayer book in his hands and reverently began the committal service.

"Dearly beloved…" he began.

Their voices rising in the clear air, the men sang a capella: *Oh, boundless Salvation, deep ocean of love. Oh, fullness of mercy, Christ brought from above.*

Then, reading from the Prayers of the Dear Departed, and inserting Michael Ernest Shepard and David Chamberlain into the name spaces, the two men committed the images of their earthly remains to the depths of the sea. With nooses about the stiff necks of their effigies and the beckoning call of the weights fighting the buoyancy of the wood, the sailors swung the plywood men softly, feet first, into the water where they slipped noiselessly beneath into the fathomless deep.

At three miles an hour traveling downward in the sea, the men calculated that their effigies would not touch the bottom until one hour later. By that time, the wood would be compressed into the thickness of a dime and their sins likewise diminished.

Having now between them the cleanest of unburdened souls, the men felt they had fulfilled their own theology and believed their sins buried in the ocean by a loving God. Dave and Shep embraced each other -- the dearest friend they would ever know -- and wept.

Returning the Book of Prayer to its shelf, Shep set the kettle to boil and began preparations for the evening meal, while the sound of Dave's tin whistle, piping away at some ancient mariner's song, wafted from the deck.

37
Homecoming

By his calculations, Dave estimated Mini and her two-man crew were about four hundred miles from Hilo. Both men were so impatient to reach land that the electricity almost visibly bounced off their skin. At about three hundred miles from shore, in preparation for landfall, they began jettisoning provisions they hadn't used, tossing extra water, crackers, and other sea-friendly items overboard, not least of which was Mini's wooden rudder. Realizing it would never again be attached to the little ship, the men carved their names, the date, and miles traveled point-to-point in its shiny mahogany side, and set it adrift in the gentle wake off the stern, knowing there was a likelihood it could make land in some secluded Hawaiian cove.

"Who knows?" Shep laughed, "Some year, ages and ages hence, we might happen onto it hanging on the wall of some obscure tavern, or maybe even in a maritime museum."

But inside Mini's cabin was a permanent memento of the trip. For the past week, Dave had carefully been carving, "Pacific Crossing. Dave and Shep. Chula Vista to Hilo. May '92. 2,550 miles," into the berth header at the front of the cabin. Chiseled into the shiny polyurethaned wood there would also eventually be a sketch of Mini in full rigging, her mast bearing the cross and dove. Then beneath, "1967" "Mini" -- her birth date.

After sailing through the night, on the morning of May 28, at the first sign of sunrise and early into Shep's watch, he set the ritual coffee to boil. The men expected to see the island soon. They anxiously watched the horizon for hours, drinking mugs of hot coffee and talking, sailing on and on. Then, not realizing he was seeing the sulphur steam vapor coming off the top of the Mauna Loa volcano, Shep spotted Hilo.

"What's that?" he asked, shielding his eyes against the sun glare.

"There it is!" Dave yelled.

Laughing and celebrating, the two pointed again and again to the speck on the horizon and checked and re-checked the compass.

"We're going right into the harbor," Shep shouted.

"Celestial navigation is taking us directly into Hilo," Dave grinned, proud and relieved that his difficult and tedious calculations had worked.

Still seventy miles out, they were approaching land at a mere four knots per hour. Doing the math, they realized they wouldn't arrive until evening.

"'So close yet so far away,' takes on new meaning from the vantage point of a boat," Dave mused.

Grabbing the cleaning supplies, the two spent all that day scrubbing salt from Mini's surfaces, polishing the green oxidized patina off her brass fittings and generally tidying up. Over the radio, they could hear the coastguard asking if the small sailing vessel out that way might be in distress. A new pleasure -- from that distance the two could talk to land.

"We're from the sailing vessel Mini," Dave radioed in. "We are doing well and expect to make landfall by late afternoon."

Hearing the first human voice other than their own after thirty days, made them feel they were already ashore.

Ever meticulous, Dave shaved, splashed on some Old Spice and prepared to make land. Slovenly, but dramatic Shep, sporting a brush of thick brown beard, merely joined Dave in shampooing his hair. Mr. Scruffy decided to follow the lead of Robinson Crusoe and donned a canvas bag with a hole cut in the neck and tied on his sea-worn shorts with a rope belt, preferring to come into dock looking like he'd been at sea for a good long time. But one thing the men shared. They'd both lost about twenty pounds, not just from the unpalatable MREs, but from the resistance of moving about a boat in a breeze. It was the ideal exercise.

Tensions were rising. Shep was pacing like a cat waiting for supper. Dave calmly relished these last few moments. After all, they'd sailed the ocean blue for thirty days and thousands of miles, tacking literally three-hundred miles up and three-hundred miles back at a time, as well as side to side to catch the winds. So, though the actual distance from California to Hawaii was only 2,200 miles, the Mini and her small crew had sailed more than 2,500.

Finally, Dave pulled out the little Seagull motor that had been lying in salt since the storm. It was the worst engine in the world, but had the distinction of being hand-built by a single worker in England. Though certainly not top of the line, the small engine was a gift from Shep to Dave and he liked the quaintness of its origins. Not surprisingly, it wouldn't start, the moisture having seeped into the cylinder.

Non-plussed, Dave removed the plugs and proceeded to blow out the engine and rub alcohol into its stubborn parts. A good three hours later, the little engine finally fired up. About ten miles from shore, with a small ceremonial flourish, Dave poured the last of the gasoline, which they'd been saving for just this moment, into the little top tank, set the throttle on high and began to motor into Hilo. The splashing of the ocean intensified against Mini's side, accompanied now by the unfamiliar and constant hum of the motor. But it wasn't long before Dave, sailing-purist-nearing-land that he was, pulled in the motor, hoisted Mini's well-used sails and under wind power alone sailed proudly into Hilo State Park, running Mini aground at full speed into the soft white sand.

Dave and Shep jumped gamely off the boat and for the first time in a month, savored the sweet sensation of land beneath their feet.

A local fireman, picnicking with his family on the Hilo beach, watched as Mini came in from open sea rather than from around the horn where most boats appear.

"Wait a minute," he said aloud. "This boat isn't from the islands, it's come from the mainland."

Others looked up in surprise. They began straggling to the water by twos and threes, gathering to see what this strange apparition could be.

As Dave and Shep walked slowly up the beach, their land legs wobbly, the small crowd began circling the men, slapping them on the back, inquiring as to their wellbeing and offering to treat them to meals and hospitality at the end of their amazing journey. Much like their send-off, it seemed that something about their sailing adventure had captured people's imagination.

"I'm home, Eva," Dave almost whispered into the first onshore phone he could find.

Dave knew Eva would not be at Hilo for his landing. They'd agreed before he sailed that would be best. Simply hearing his voice and knowing he was safe and would be home soon was enough for her. Steady as the rock of Gibraltar, Eva's faith that her husband would cross the immensity of the unknown and return to her safely was a matter of belief.

"I'm glad. I love you," Eva whispered back.

Shep had no such assurance of his wife's emotional temperature. Their marriage might remain tenuous at this point, but his love for her was not. As he scanned the crowd on the sunlit shore he was looking for the one face he wanted more than any other to see. It was not there. With sagging shoulders he turned away, but not before a sudden movement at the back of the throng caught his eye. Shep's heart skipped a beat as the ever-so-familiar shape of his wife moved toward him through the soft Hawaiian sand. The fingers of her left hand rested gently on her forehead, an old signal between them that he understood -- she loves me still.

As if on cue, the two seafaring men turned toward each other and hugged tightly.

We did it, their eyes said to each other. *We did it.*

Shep reached into his sea bag and pulled out his harness, dulled now by salt and wear, and held it out to Dave.

"I want you to have this. It really wasn't my harness. You were."

Dave smiled. "Well, I don't need two, so here's mine," he said, placing his in his friend's hand and wrapping it with his own.

The Crossing had been what they always thought it would be -- an affirmation of their faith, of life itself, and of their friendship.

As Dave turned back toward Mini, their small companion over the long trek, Shep slung his duffle over his shoulder and walked up the beach to the waiting arms of his wife.

Shep's final log entry:

"Someday some boy may ask me, 'Sir, are you a real sailor?' No, I'll reply. But I once crossed an ocean with one."

ACKNOWLEDGEMENTS

My sincere gratitude to all the wonderful friends and family members who've encouraged me through this long process, read endless drafts, made suggestions, and kept me going. To Walt Mendelson for invaluable tips on publishing and for the original cover. To Jim Willoughby for his unflagging belief in my ability, and to Ray Newton, my writing mentor. Also, love and thanks to my biggest supporter, my husband Mike "Shep" Shepard, who never gave up on me, or on this project. Lastly, but certainly not least, gigantic thanks to Dave Chamberlain and Shep for this wonderful story and for their willingness to give up any shred of privacy to make it as true as possible to their great adventure.

EPILOGUE

Dave Chamberlain still owns Mini and sails her regularly, though closer to home. He is a retired pastor with The Christian and Missionary Alliance and actively involved with the church he founded. He is a gigging jazz trombonist, a piano technician, and continues to be a prolific music inventor with his company, Chasons Music. Dave still lives in Chula Vista, California, with the wife of his youth and the love of his life, Eva.

Mike "Shep" Shepard returned to his hometown of Prescott, Arizona, where he lives with his wife and the author of this book, Sandy Moss. He is very active in the community and in his work with the Prescott Unified School District. He counts his years of service with The Salvation Army as profoundly shaping. Through the ensuing years, he's had a repetitive dream in which he is among his Salvation Army comrades, but always unable to locate a uniform.

Made in the USA
San Bernardino, CA
30 May 2016